Dr Marny Lishman is a health and community psychologist, author, wellbeing and mindset coach, keynote speaker, media commentator and 9 News Perth's resident psychologist.

She holds a Bachelor of Psychology and a Doctor of Psychology, with health and community psychology speciality titles.

Marny helps people increase their psychological capacity to create the life they want, while dealing with the inevitable disruptions they will face on their path to success. An animal lover who requires lots of sunlight and time in nature, she is her best self when she can go on long daily beach walks with her dog, indulge in reading books, meditate and spend time with her shiny (but rather loud) children.

Burnout to Brilliant

A practical guide to recharging, resetting and redesigning your life

DR MARNY LISHMAN

First published by Affirm Press in 2024
Boon Wurrung Country
28 Thistlethwaite Street
South Melbourne, VIC 3205
affirmpress.com.au

10 9 8 7 6 5 4 3 2 1

A catalogue record for this book is available from the National Library of Australia

ISBN: 9781922848505 (paperback)

Cover design by Alissa Dinallo © Affirm Press
Author photograph by Natasha Dupreez
Typeset in 11/17 pt Adobe Text Pro by Post Pre-press Group, Brisbane
Printed and bound in China by C&C Offset Printing Co. Ltd.

While this is a work of nonfiction, some names and identifying details have been changed to protect the privacy of the people involved.

To my loves – Lali & Luca xxx

Contents

Introduction

'Healing is a matter of time,
but it is sometimes also a
matter of opportunity.'

HIPPOCRATES

THIS PAST YEAR I've needed water. I don't mean that I've been excessively thirsty, or that my doctor has told me I'm not drinking enough fluids or I'm not meeting the recommended eight glasses of water a day. Nor is it that I've been noticing more wrinkles on my face lately (well, not really).

I mean that I've had an intense need to be *in* water. Like a calling, an urge, a desire to be in, on or under water. Floating, swimming, bathing, sitting or just bobbing around in it. Not just a quick mindless water experience that I, and probably most of us, engage in daily. It's almost a feeling of being pulled by my mind and body to water to be soothed and more connected to the present moment. Because once immersed, I feel a shift, a whisper from my body that this is where it needs me to be, even just for a moment. A small reset, refresh and recharge that fills up something inside of me again – something that was so near depletion only moments before.

Loving water is nothing new to me, but perhaps over the past few years I'd forgotten how much I loved it (and needed it). A side effect of developing into an adult, for many of us, unfortunately often involves a slow shedding of the innately pleasurable activities that once took up so much of our time as children. Parallel to us growing older, moving through our teenage years into adulthood and one by one taking on more societal roles, there's a quiet tapering off of the hobbies we once loved, often without us even noticing. And along with this, there's a disappearance of possibilities of who we might have become if we continued them.

Being a 'nature child' who is energised by natural spaces, I've always been at home around water. I'd spend hours of my day as a child swimming at the beach near my home. Those were the days when beach life was simple; before families started taking 'luggage' to the beach. It was long before the mandatory beach cabanas, bags, chairs, towels, hats, carts, mats, drink bottles and having to pack 50 million snacks to keep the family happy. In those days, kids would go to the beach with nothing but the idea of a frolic and some fun. We'd swim all day in the sun without even a thought. Dangerously, we'd swim in huge morning swells that dumped our bodies onto the beach with bather bottoms full of sloppy sand lumps, and swim in the choppy murky afternoon currents that pulled us hundreds of metres down the beach. All the while our parents sunbaked obliviously on the beach, without noticing that we'd floated literally into another beachside suburb.

I'm drawn to water, but I've never felt the yearning to be immersed in it as much as I have this past year. Being a psychologist and reasonably reflective human being I, of course, can't help but try to analyse why this has been so. Maybe it's because I worked nonstop with clients right up until Christmas Eve, which is something us psychologists often do because Christmas isn't exactly the most joyous time of the year for many people. Maybe it's because I didn't take much time off work to recharge and reset over the holiday season. Maybe it's because I haven't had a proper holiday for a few years. Maybe it's because of unprocessed grief from yet another loved one passing away. Maybe it's because of a recent cancer diagnosis for my beloved cat. Maybe it's because of the daily coordination and caring for my elderly, unwell parent. Maybe it's the result of an excessive workload that is sometimes a little hard to keep up with. Maybe it's because of ongoing demands on my time from the too many hats I wear. Maybe it's because every single night of the week has been spent driving teenagers to all their sports trainings. Maybe it's because I feel that I keep letting people down because it's impossible for me to be in three or four places at the same time. Maybe it's because of certain people I have been working with who've been causing me undue pressure. Maybe it's perimenopause knocking at the door and my body temperature giving me a prelude of what's to come. Maybe it's pandemic fatigue creeping in. Maybe it was simply because summer was just so hot. Maybe it's because of all of it. But whatever the cause, I needed to be underwater. A lot.

Once I'd taken that swim, I felt calmer. A sense of vitality washed over me and I felt more at ease. We can be emotionally driven creatures, us human beings, and being in the water allowed me a moment to stop, reflect and shift to a positive emotional state again. Everything that day became better because of it. I'm no Wim Hof, but the small water rituals to re-energise myself have continued.

If we were all more honest with ourselves and slowed down a little, it's likely we would notice that our minds and bodies are whispering something to us. They may be telling us we need to do things a little differently, adjust some behaviours accordingly, so that we can feel better in moments we're in distress. And if we'd only stop and listen, we'd get the valuable information about what we need to be doing (or not doing) to soothe ourselves. But many of us don't listen. We don't stop to notice the stressors, the pressures or the feelings. Instead, we just keep going – for days, weeks, months and years – slowly becoming someone we're not. In doing so, we miss the valuable information that is being whispered to us by the parts of us that know us best. These insights are designed to help steer us in a better direction that is aligned with a better suited life.

Maybe our exhaustion is telling us to slow down. Maybe our tiredness is telling us that 14-hour days are excessive. Maybe our aching body is telling us we shouldn't be sitting down all day in front of a computer. Maybe our sleeplessness is telling us to have a conversation with our boss about our impossible workload. Maybe our irritability in the morning is telling us to ease off on the evening wines. Maybe our unhappiness is telling us how out of alignment we are with our career. Maybe the feelings of dread we experience are telling us to stay away from someone. Maybe the heart palpitations are telling us to learn how to manage our anxiety. Maybe our sluggishness is telling us to spend more time in nature. Maybe our heavy shoulders are telling us we're feeling overwhelmed. Maybe the endless colds are telling us that we're worn out and we need some help.

Maybe we need a break. Maybe we need to quit. Maybe we need to do the thing that we've aways really wanted to do. Maybe we need to say 'no' to people more often. Maybe we need to say 'yes' to ourselves more often. Maybe our emotions need to be felt, for the first time in a long time.

To be processed. To be learned from. To use as a catalyst for changing our life. Maybe we've been here. Maybe we're there. Maybe we don't ever want to get there.

It's hard to know what we need to do next when we're burned out. Once we've reached the tipping point into the realm of burnout, it's hard to see the path ahead. The physical and psychological capabilities that are there to help us recover, heal and create a better life are completely turned down, or have taken a well-earned nap for a while. It's all still there – it's just, well, overused, overwhelmed and over it. It's hard to create a positive way forward in that headspace. But if we can conjure up some energy to learn from our reflections and curiosity as to how and why we got to this burnout point, the insight we gain can lead to something bigger and better for our life in the future.

After the psychological and physical exhaustion phase of burnout, once we pause for a while and start to recharge again, something of value comes from the experience. In fact, something very valuable. Much like all life adversities, individual and collective, going through burnout is often a transformative experience. Burnout hits our psyche so hard that it becomes a powerful catalyst for change; it's the dark night of the soul that we didn't think we needed. If we listen to the messages it brings, and we put those learnings to good use, a massive psychological pivot can occur. It's a shedding of the old and a creating of the new, with a firm intention to not live like we once did.

It involves a 'knowing' about what caused us to burn out in the first place. Perhaps it's a result of a lack of support from our 'people' when trying to raise our children. Perhaps it's a result of not speaking up about the overwhelm in our psychologically unsafe workplace. Perhaps it's a result of a micromanaging line manager who wore us down. Perhaps it's a result of our people-pleasing behaviours that meant we've been constantly saying 'no' to ourselves. Perhaps it's a lack of control in our relationship that has been building up for some time. Perhaps our job compromised our values. Perhaps we've been doing too much of what we thought we 'should', rather than what we truly wanted. Perhaps our excessive workload was impossibly ridiculous or maybe it was boringly tedious. Perhaps it was because we're a workaholic and have no idea how to stop, or perhaps it's because the expectations on us were greater that we could provide. Perhaps it's because this fast-paced, modern world doesn't allow us the space to stop ... and listen. Perhaps it's because this fast-paced, modern world has a lot of things just blatantly wrong.

If we 'operationalise' burnout recovery a bit more (and get excited about it), it may involve talking, debriefing, connecting, letting go, reframing and challenging. It may involve crying, screaming, shaking, laughing or thumping our fist into the wall. It will definitely involve exercising, sleeping, meditating, fuelling our body with the right foods and spending time doing things we love. It will involve having courageous and sometimes uncomfortable conversations or setting ninja-style boundaries. It may involve quitting or it may involve starting. It may mean saying 'no' more or saying 'yes' more. It may involve being brave or being scared. It might involve more loving or maybe even leaving. It may involve just saying, 'I surrender.'

Burnout recovery is about finding ourselves again (because, let's face it, we probably disappeared for a while), meeting ourselves where we need to be and giving ourselves what we need to function at our best. It may involve jumping in some water like me when life gets tough. It might even involve being as far away from water as we can possibly get. Who knows? Whatever it is, it's up to us to find out.

I've worked with and talked to hundreds of people throughout my career who have experienced burnout and healed from it. I've been immersed in stories of what burnout feels like, where it can stem from and, from my own professional training and experience, discovered what is crucial to recover from it. I've psychologically poked and prodded my clients and assisted them in the discovery of why they may be feeling the way they feel. I've helped them to unlock the possible reasons as to why they are suffering in the present. Most importantly, I've learned what we need to incorporate into our lives to help us thrive, even in tough times, and create more fulfilling lives with no room for burnout.

Navigating the burnout experience and coming out the other side of it better than ever involves considering where our burnout came from, challenging ourselves to do life a little differently and committing to a new way of living. That's why I've included considerations at the end of each chapter. I urge you to take the time to stop, reflect, ponder and write notes on where you've come from, why you may be feeling a certain way, where you want to go and what you are going to do starting now. These considerations will help you design what life is going to look like for you going forward. The Burnout Blueprint at the end of the book will allow you to get clear on what you want to work on, why you want to work on it, what actions you need to take and what support you need to create a mentally healthier life. It will help you articulate what needs to happen for you to come back from burnout ... better than ever.

Burnout is the wake-up call we never thought we needed. And even better, it will help us create a personal and professional life that will be better than it ever was before. Even for those who haven't experienced burnout per se, learning how to heal from burnout is still extremely helpful. The cure is often in the cause – so taking the time to reflect on how we operate in the world now, tweak it a little if required and then steer ourselves in a direction that better aligns with who we are will help us design a life that's better than we ever thought possible.

As Albert Einstein famously said, 'A clever person solves a problem. A wise person avoids it.' Let's do both.

PART 1

Burning Out

Burnout

'There is one consolation in being sick; and that is the possibility that you may recover to a better state than you were ever in before.'

HENRY DAVID THOREAU

WHEN MY SON, Luca, was three, he referred to everything that he couldn't quite find the correct words for as a 'something else', pronounced at the time as 'summon' else'. Learning the right words for things takes time, and Luca, even way back then, had a knack for life hacking. If there's an easier way of doing things, he will do it. So, if he couldn't quite articulate what an item was or couldn't find it in his vocabulary, he quite aptly referred to it as a 'something else'. If I asked what he wanted for a snack, he would reply, 'Something else'. If I asked him what game he wanted to play, he said, 'Something else'. If I asked him what movie he wanted to watch, he said, 'Something else'. If I asked him what he was up to, of course, it was 'Something else'. One of his brightly coloured paintings even came home with him from kindergarten one afternoon with his teacher's writing in the top corner noting the artist's name and description of the artwork: 'Something Else' by Luca.

Fast forward a decade and whenever my kids and

I encounter weird phenomena – events, situations, objects and even difficult people – that are indescribable, we still crack ourselves up by referring to them as a 'something else'. It's our own joke that no one else gets. Well, burnout is something else.

People bandy around the term 'burnout' a lot these days. The term is used mainly when people are describing an extreme exhaustion that they are experiencing in relation to something or many things that are stressing them out in the context of their life. It's a term that writers like to pair with an image of a line of matches, with a fully lit match at the beginning of a row and a series of matches following that are slowing burning down to nearly nothing. And for those who have experienced burnout, that image is quite accurately personified – a person who once felt whole, active, luminous and shiny is now reduced to feeling fragmented, languid, dark and dull, as though they have no energy remaining to operate. Their light has gone.

Burnout was included in the 11th Revision of the World Health Organization's International Classification of Diseases (ICD-11) in 2019 as a purely occupational phenomenon. This demonstrates the seriousness of the condition and its apparent rise in recent times. Burnout is described in the ICD-11 as 'a syndrome conceptualised as resulting from chronic workplace stress that has not been successfully managed' and is characterised 'by three dimensions which include the feelings of energy depletion of exhaustion, the increased mental distance and negative feelings for one's occupational context and the subsequent reduced professional efficacy that results'.[1]

The recent ICD-11 definition states that burnout specifically refers to phenomena in the occupational context and that it should not be applied to describe experiences in other areas of life. But we're most definitely going to be applying it to all other areas of life in this book. The sum of our parts makes a whole. Our reactions to the goings-on and not-goings-on in each area of our life are inextricably linked, whether we want them to be or not when we're burned out. The same brain is operating in all these areas. We can't take our brain out and put another one in depending on the day. It's not a jacket. We're sentient beings who are in a constant state of absorbing what's going on in our changing environments. As the old proverb goes, 'Wherever you go, there you are', and that's the same with our experience of burnout. Wherever our brain is, whatever it is perceiving, whatever it is feeling, however it is guiding us to behave and however it leads us to interact with the world ... oh, there we are. Burnout is about everything. And burnout can be experienced by anyone.

Burnout is a psychological syndrome emerging from a

prolonged response to chronic stressors in the context of a person's life. It's a state of mental, emotional and physical exhaustion that has emerged because of an individual's stress response in their nervous system being continually on alert as though they, as a human being, are constantly under threat. There is a wide variety of symptoms of burnout that a sufferer would know all too well, once they realise what it is. But the thing is, this 'realisation' often doesn't happen for a while, and it's only with hindsight that people can recollect their burnout signals and where it all started. This is because this burnout business is often operating covertly, slowing building up before it slaps us in the face.

So, given we might not know we have it nor be leading up to it, how on earth can we prevent it (or stop it from happening again)? We don't just wake up one morning with burnout. We certainly don't get a little sniffle of tiredness and grab a rapid antigen test out of our medicine cabinet to check if we're burnout positive. Sometimes we may have it without even realising. Burnout often sneaks up on us over time. We may have been too busy to notice, or we've been operating in that way for so long that we've become the embodiment of burnout. In any case, our brain and body are out of alignment, in a dis-eased state. They are telling us something is awry, and probably have been telling us for a while. So, let's start listening.

Mental, physical, emotional and spiritual exhaustion is the overarching theme of burnout. It's an umbrella of exhaustion that covers myriad internal symptoms that slowly start appearing over time and then show up in our behaviours, which can affect all the different facets of our life and affect everything externally. It stuffs up our emotions, stunts our intellect, confuses our logic, disconnects us from those we love, makes us sick, sabotages our goals and talks us into giving up on our dreams. It can even make us want to die. Yes, seriously.

Burnout doesn't always happen because of heaps of things or massive amounts of anything. It can come about because of our experience of lots of things or one thing. Burnout is not caused solely by work environments or too many personal responsibilities loading up on us. We don't have to have a Beyoncé-esque concert line-up or the schedule of the Prime Minister to become burned out. The main stipulation is that burnout can be experienced by anyone with prolonged levels of chronic stress, emotional build-up and pressure causing overwhelm, and these feelings can be caused by many factors.[2] No one is totally immune. Sole parents, single parents and a parent with a partner can get burned out.[3] People without children can get burned out. Teenagers can get burned out. Organisational employees and their leaders can get burned out. Musicians, actors, athletes, entrepreneurs and artists can get burned out. Caregivers, carers and students can get burned out. Teachers, doctors, nurses and vets can get burned out.[4] Psychologists can get burned out. This one nearly did.

There are many complicated definitions out there for burnout. At its simplest level, burnout is about feelings. Becoming burned out occurs because we're not being guided by our feelings, and that happens for a variety of reasons. Feelings are 100 per cent valid for us at the time, but they're often not channelled in the correct way for us to make them useful. This is through no fault of our own (well, mostly). That said, a lot of us can do *a lot* better in learning to work with our feelings. But this is why we're here, right?

Feeling the Feels

'Feeling all your feelings is
hard, but that's what they're for.
Feelings are for feeling.
All of them. Even the hard ones.'

GLENNON DOYLE

A FEELING IS an experience of emotion. It is a conscious and subjective experience of emotion that, given a particular situation or event, might make us react differently to others around us. That's why our mates, family and our neighbour down the street feel and behave a little differently after something occurs, even when the contextual experience is the same. As I write this paragraph, my dog Chilly is sitting next me. I'm expecting a package to arrive today and when the postman knocks on the door, my feeling (excitement about yet another book delivery ... yay) is going to be very different to Chilly's feeling (alarm about the door knock by the postman, who she hates). Same event, different interpretation, different feelings and likely to be very different behaviours (me skipping to the door, Chilly acting excessively cautious).

Our feelings motivate us to do things in life. They help us behave in certain ways and direct our actions to get more of the 'good' feelings, or away from some of the 'bad' feelings. We might study to feel smarter, we might work harder to feel important, we might go to the gym to feel more confident, we might wear red lipstick to feel more attractive and we might hop on a dating app to feel loved. We might also end a relationship to stop feeling so controlled, we might go to sleep earlier to stop feeling tired and we might cut down our hours at work so we don't feel so busy or rushed.

Feelings can be physical, too. We might put on a jumper to feel warm, grab a drink to feel satiated or get a massage to feel relaxed. We tend to do better at the physical feelings side of things, but for the feelings-as-an-expression-of-emotion side of things, let's just say we're works in progress. And when I say works in progress, I mean there's a lot of work to be done in that department for a lot of us.

As I mentioned, a feeling is an experience of emotion. Emotions are powerful. They are giving us valuable information about our environment in the present moment. We are supposed to feel the full range of emotions as we walk on our own life journey and then do something about them when we're feeling them. After that, we are supposed to move on with our business, of course with the learnings of what the emotions taught us about our environment. Emotions are crucial for our survival, and in modern times, we don't take them seriously enough. In fact, many of us ignore them.

Thirty-thousand years ago, our ancestors would have been walking along the savannah, carrying out their duties while constantly tuning in to what was going on in their environment. They obviously didn't have locks on doors, alarms to notify them when there was an emergency or other safety systems, which many of us are privileged to have in our lives today. I'm pretty sure there weren't any 'Beware of Lions' signs along the savannah tracks back then, nor were there news reports of the local 'Neanderthal gang' breaking into caves again. Our ancestors relied on their finely tuned senses to give them the information they needed from their environment. If they were walking along the savannah with their pack, a predator crossing their path would have elicited a stress response in the brain and nervous system before any rational thought took place. Within milliseconds, the emotion of fear would have been felt and a chain of psychological and physical events to optimise their chance for survival – to fight or flee – would have been set off. Their senses would have brought in valuable information about the threat in front of them, with the brain then focusing all its resources on that threat; the heart directing blood to the limbs, adrenal glands pumping adrenaline and cortisol through their veins and the turning down of bodily functions that were secondary for survival.

Those who didn't feel scared or fearful in those moments would have mostly been killed. The 'feeling' of these emotions was crucial for our survival back then and we've adapted to have the psychological capabilities to feel these emotions now. We would not be here today without them. The emotions that we perceive as 'negative' and that we so often find uncomfortable to feel were critical for us to stay alive, and that's why we have them today. It's not only fear and stress that are important, but myriad other emotions such as anger, shame, regret, sadness, guilt and disgust, and they need to be felt. As uncomfortable as our feelings can be, they are telling us important things about our emotions and interpreting the information that is arising from our environment.

In the lead-up to burnout, we've often been feeling a lot of those negative (but very necessary) emotions, repetitively, for a long time. Yet we may not have felt them to their fullest. We've likely been pushing through them, denying, ignoring or even rationalising them. Whatever we did with those emotions, we didn't use them the way emotions are meant to be used. We didn't feel them like they needed to be felt. We denied ourselves of the powerful information about what wasn't working for us in our environment, and what we needed to do to feel at ease again.

Many of us are not emotionally agile enough in our

modern world (through no fault of our own). We're not using our emotions for what they are meant to be used for. If we're feeling an emotion and not doing anything about it, it stays inside of us for longer than it should. Bundle a few emotions together, all of which are not shifting, and what we're left with is a big hotchpotch of emotions that are untouched, unprocessed, unresolved and mixed together like a big soup of despair that is wearing us out. Unfortunately, by this stage, we often have no ounce of energy to get the strainer out to make sense of it all. So yes, there are many reasons why we get burned out, but before we get into them (and out of them), let's look at what that hot pot of burnout looks like, and feels like.

American singer-songwriter Michael Gungor wrote, 'Burnout is what happens when you try to avoid being human for too long.' Not a truer word has been spoken about burnout. We are human, and us humans need to feel, but most of us are not operating in a way that allows us to be how we have evolved to be. Modern society is also not conducive to this. We need to feel our emotions fully. Otherwise, they build up and not only exhaust us, but can cause further emotional havoc, guiding us in life directions away from who we truly are.

Emotionally, people experiencing burnout report feeling a real dissatisfaction with life and often struggle to feel happiness in any areas of their life anymore (even if the main cause of dissatisfaction originates in a single area). If you've ever felt chronically stressed as a result of what's going on in the workplace, it's likely you will feel stressed at home too. The feeling of unrelenting stress and overwhelming pressure is common with burnout, and some experience a sadness or emptiness they can't explain. On top of this, feelings of anxiety or dread are (more often than not) present, with a sense of panic that takes over on occasion. It's like our nervous system is operating on high alert and it doesn't take too much to set it off (which, from a neuroscience point of view, is true). In this state, people feel like they have nothing left to give to anyone or anything.

Another thing about a nervous system living on the edge is it's going to be creating a more irritated, angry, impatient person with a very short fuse. And if those emotions don't shift, it is likely to move to feeling cynical, jaded or even contemptuous. A few years ago, I had a client who couldn't stand any of his co-workers at all. Like, *at all*. He'd worked with them for 15 years; they'd gone to university together undertaking the same degree and they'd been friends for a long time. But this was all changing because of work pressures and unresolved occupational issues. When pressed (by me, of course) to explore some of his colleagues' favourable characteristics, he could not find one iota of positivity in any of the people he had spent nine hours a day with for years. Not one. There was simply nothing left there for him to see anymore, nor any desire to reconnect. He was emotionally done with work and his workmates.

Emotions also have the power (if not felt properly and used to benefit us) to sneakily manifest into physical symptoms and illness. Pretty much everyone who has experienced burnout has felt exhaustion. And it's not the type of exhaustion that can be solved by going to bed earlier and having a good night's sleep to make up for it. It's next-level fatigue that feels as though there's not an ounce of fuel left for you to operate your brain or your body.

Feeling detached, isolated and almost dissociated from real life is common, along with a disconnection from your identity. Some people have described their experience as looking down on themselves from high above, outside of their own body, watching themselves go through the motions without any feeling. One of my clients felt he was just 'not there' anymore and we joked (yes, even in low points, my clients and I can find moments to crack a joke) that he had become 'the artist formerly known as' Scott. He believed he was destined to become a symbol next if we didn't embark on a new journey – a journey to find out who he was (which, of course, we did).

When we don't cope with perceived threats in a helpful way, our brain will lure us into easing the emotional pain in an unhelpful way. Our brain isn't fussy when we've had the life drained out of us – that's why people who are burned out often make things worse by misusing substances such as drugs and alcohol. This may make us feel better for a moment, but it will inevitably make things worse in the long run. Many of my clients have told me their excessive drinking behaviours emerged around the time of feeling relentless stress. In an attempt to self-soothe, they reach for the familiar thing that they know makes them feel good – a reasonably common 'solution' for those in burnout.

Burnout also has the tendency to completely disrupt sleep. The most irrational thing about burnout is that sleep is what people with burnout want the most, but it's something they often can't get enough of. Sleep can be inconsistent, with sleeping too much at the wrong times and being unable to sleep at the right times common occurrences. It may start out as trouble falling asleep, or waking at 2am engaging with a monkey mind of unnecessary worry and rumination. Burnout causes sleep chaos at a time when we're at our most tired, leaving us not wanting to get out from under the duvet in the morning.

Mentally, people experiencing burnout feel like they've 'checked out'. They have no interest in the things they once loved nor the motivation to even think about them. They often can't be bothered anymore in the workplace and are not as productive in their personal roles at home or in the community. They can't focus, their brain feels foggy and they can't problem-solve, come up with new ideas or make decisions. Mistakes become common as well as negative feedback from family, friends, employers and colleagues who are witnessing their dwindling energy and enthusiasm, along with their performance of usual duties and tasks taking a nosedive. Cognitively, everything is interpreted negatively and adds to the existing negative mindset.

And, of course, who's going to have fun when they're constantly fighting or fleeing a lion in their minds? None of us. Everything becomes big, overwhelming and serious. There's no fun to be had when we're burned out. A sense of hopelessness, helplessness, failure and self-doubt will also put a stop to any chance of having fun.

Physically, people who are burned out are more vulnerable to colds and flus (hey, if we're not taking a break, our immune system might) and even flare-ups of once-dormant diseases.[5] If we've got any of the myriad autoimmune conditions, this will resonate. Autoimmune conditions, like an annoying uninvited house guest, often like to come and say 'hello' when we're psychologically depleted.[6]

Unexplainable aches and pains often increase, plus the resurrection of old injuries.[7] It's intriguing to me, as a health psychologist, how many people's backs 'go out' when they've been in emotional distress for too long. A negative bonus (if we can call it that) might even be a new injury. It seems that we become more accident-prone when burned out, as we don't tend to be fully present when we're engaging in activities. Other times, people might get an injury or an illness out of the blue that seems (at the time) to be quite unexplainable (but yes, with hindsight, is very explainable given the burnout that was creeping in). A couple of years ago, when I was feeling under pressure and very overwhelmed, my right shoulder decided to just lock itself up – it froze shut. It just stopped doing what a shoulder is supposed to do. I woke up one morning and it didn't want to move up or down or out – at all. It went on *for a whole year.* There's nothing like a frozen shoulder, agonising pain and an inability to shave under your armpit to force you to slow down. I'm still recovering as I write this, and I still can't do a full YMCA dance routine to this day.

Avoidance behaviours are also common in people who are burned out. This can range from people not coming into work to extreme procrastination,[8] not being able to communicate to people, not wanting to see certain friends or do anything else that involves deep thinking. It's all too much. Thinking about, fantasising about or even making big changes can also be common (without the necessary 'thinking through', which is often needed to make a well-informed decision) without it being the 'right' decision. This may involve some form of quitting (relationships, work, friendships),[9] completely switching careers, moving house to another city or even some other extreme lifestyle change to remove the person from their current situation.Anything to avoid or run away in the hope that they will *feel* differently. As Snagglepuss, the sassy Hanna-Barbera cartoon cat, would say, we feel like we want to 'exit, stage left'. And some of us do and regret it later when we're feeling better.

Spiritually, we are disconnected. We often feel lost, disconnected from anything bigger than ourselves and, even more importantly, disconnected from our higher self. Time and time again, I have heard the same statement from people experiencing burnout: they don't even know who they are anymore. They feel out of alignment and totally lost. They feel like something is amiss, but their brain is so laser focused on what's going wrong that they can't see the bigger picture.

It's safe to say we feel emotionally, mentally, physically and spiritually discombobulated when we're burned out. And, in a weird way, this is supposed to happen.

What's Stress Got to Do With It?

'Man needs difficulties;
they are necessary for health.'

CARL JUNG

I'M SURE YOU'RE familiar with the following phrases. 'I'm stressed out.' 'This is stressing me out.' 'Don't stress me out.' 'This is so stressful.' If you've ever yelled, 'When is this going to end?!' or, in today's acronym-dense language, 'WTF' when faced with yet another life struggle to tackle, you know what stress feels like. This type of stress rhetoric reflects a state of emotional strain that feels like a cross between overwhelm and pressure, with some uneasiness thrown in for good measure. In its simplest description, burnout happens because of this type of unrelenting stress, or stress that doesn't shift after a period of time. Among the myriad other feelings and emotions involved in the burning-out process, stress is likely to be the dominant feeling, which means it needs special attention, and therefore its own special chapter.

The term 'stressed' is usually used as an adjective to describe an emotional reaction to something (the stressor) or many things (stressors) that are happening to a person. We can be feeling stressed because of the pressure of a looming deadline, because of a rather large bill we don't have the money to pay, because of our toddler flinging spaghetti all over the wall or because of being micromanaged in our job. We can also feel stressed because of multiple stressors or daily hassles existing at the same time across the many areas of our life: being stuck in traffic on the school run, having conflict with our partner, caring for a sick parent, dealing with a psychologically unsupportive manager or all the micro tasks involved in looking after children. So, stress can be felt as a result of the cumulative effect of all of these things happening.

Burnout symptoms sound (and feel) positively awful, but they all make perfect sense from an evolutionary point of view based on the role stress plays in our survival. As previously discussed, we are supposed to feel the whole spectrum of emotions. Our aim is to observe them, be curious about them and be guided by them. The emotion of stress is one that we're not likely to ever be void of, as being engaged in life will always present us with stressors. The funny thing about stress is that even if we're happily engaged in life to its fullest, we'll likely come up with more stressors than ever. But there's an important distinction here: it's not the stress that matters, it's what we do with it that counts. If we don't do anything with the feeling of stress as we experience it, the build-up may over time result in burnout.

Human beings are made well for stress. However, we're made for acute, over-and-done-with type of stress. The emotion of stress gives us a feeling that there is something up in our environment, possibly a threat. The ancestors whose blood runs through us – who were more tuned in to the threats in the savannah, and were more attuned to their senses – not only kept more of their pack safe but kept our gene pool generating to this day. Their spritely nervous system and tendency to feel stress to its fullest and do with it what it was intended to do is the reason we are here today. Feeling stress when they encountered real threats on the savannah, such as their not-so-friendly neighbourhood lion, would have whipped them into taking the best actions necessary for their survival.

We're in a different era now, but we have the same brain mechanisms at work. The brain physiology that helped our ancestors run away from predators, and made us feel fearful of unfamiliar tribes, is now responding the same way when we encounter difficult colleagues, angry partners, traffic jams and inflation. But, unlike our ancestors, we don't often deal fully with the stressors, and the stress stays.

We're made to feel stress, and then do something with that feeling. We're not made to just meander on in a fight, flight or freeze state for days, weeks, months or years on end like too many of us do nowadays. We're not supposed to feel stress about big things going on in the context of our life without actioning them. We're not made for feeling stress about lots of little things constantly, without navigating through them to a point of resolve. We're not supposed to allow these stressors to build up, causing unnecessary pressure on our mental, emotional, physical and spiritual faculties. This is when chronic stress can morph into burnout.

Stress can be defined as any type of change we experience that causes mental, emotional or even physical strain. It's our brain detecting a difference, a change, a pressure or even a threat. It's information that we need to absorb, think about and do something with. The feeling of stress shouldn't be ignored.

But, before we get caught up in bagging stress completely and aspiring to a rather unrealistic life of no stress, we need to hold space for it. Feeling stress is helpful to us. Not only does it feed us valuable information about what's not good in our present environment so we can navigate it, but it also directs us towards things that are better for us in the future. Feeling stress keeps us alert, focused, competent and motivated to get stuff done. It can also keep us energised, interested and more creative. Without feeling stress, we would probably spend the day lying on the couch in our tracksuit being bored, eating crisps, binge-watching Netflix all day and heading towards an existential crisis. While this option may feel quite attractive right now, particularly if we are burned out, it's not what we want to be doing every day for the foreseeable future.

Stress is a natural response to life pressures and dangerous situations. The pressure can come from what's happening around us, but also from the overwhelming demands we and others often place on ourselves. In other words, sometimes it's our environment, and often it's our own choices in life that have created stress – a mix of things we sometimes can't do anything about, and some we can.

Chronic stress ends up wearing people away day after day, month after month, year after year. And this is what can lead to burnout. It's the cumulative effect of stress. The not managing it, the building up of it, the not dealing with it, the non-removing of it – the whole stinking thing. We're not supposed to just marinate in stress and do nothing about it. We're supposed to notice it, and then create change.

But much like anger, which can be a primary and a secondary emotion, stress can be caused by a build-up of other emotions. We can feel stressed because we have low self-esteem and feel low in confidence. We can feel stressed because we are fearful we can't cope with uncertainty or change. We can feel stressed because we feel controlled or trapped. We can feel stressed because we feel unfulfilled or out of alignment with the work we are doing. We can feel stressed because of lots of things going on, and we can feel stressed because not enough is going on.

In any case, as much as we try, we are not going to get rid of stress completely. So, it's a waste of time wishing and waiting for 'no stress'. Stress is part of being alive. So, we need to be grateful for our stress, because it has got us this far. It has kept us alert and given us the energy to meet the more difficult life challenges we have faced already. Let's be kind to it, appreciative of it and use it as a valuable guide for us as to what to do next.

So, now we know what burnout might feel like, and we know that stress has a lot to do with it, we can start talking about how to manage it, heal from it and ultimately make sure we design a healthy life going forward. The cure is often in the cause, so knowing what the cause is can help us manage it and prevent it from happening again.

Society and All Its Woes

'Neither the life of an individual
nor the history of a society
can be understood without
understanding both.'

C WRIGHT MILLS

THERE IS A quote, once misattributed to the famous psychotherapist Sigmund Freud, that says, 'Before diagnosing yourself with depression, make sure you are not just surrounded by assholes.' Given the modernity of the language, it's highly unlikely that it came from Freud, but given the viral nature of this quote on the internet, it seems it resonates. We all know this to be true sometimes. It's not always us that's causing the distress that we're feeling – it can be other people, and we're just reacting to them.

It's important that whenever we talk about our mental health issues, we look around a bit. Like all living creatures on Earth, our environment has a lot to do with our health – physically and psychologically. So, it's crucial that we check the environment in which we are living, including its people (meaning, our society).

Despite what popular culture coverage says of burnout, particularly in the past few years, it can't be 'fixed' with better self-care that we are solely responsible for. We can't downward-dog our way out of burnout. And while there are multiple buffering agents that we can put in place to mitigate the individual ingredients that lead to burnout (and, yes, we will be doing that), we need to be aware that there are some fundamental flaws in society that still need a considerable amount of work. Laying the blame for burnout solely on our own behaviours isn't helpful. Our society in modern times is not conducive to the management of chronic stress and, in fact, lays a rather unhealthy blueprint that is allowing burnout to thrive. If we are to have a society that assists in the prevention of burnout, and the healing from burnout, a lot needs to change.

Despite the dialogue around the topic of burnout, it is not caused solely by an individual working too much or under chronic stress for far too long. As mentioned, at its rawest, burnout is more about the person not processing, expressing or utilising their emotions in response to something (or many things) that is happening in their life or that *has* happened in their life. Maybe it's because they don't know how to process these emotions, or perhaps it's because they've been conditioned over many years not to, or maybe the context is not conducive to their emotions being felt. Whatever the case may be, the emotions inevitably build up and deplete the individual's resources – burning them out. The key words here are important – 'conditioning' and 'context' – and they often have a lot to do with burnout.

Our ancestors had proficient brains and nervous systems that used emotions to whip them into action. So, how did it come about that modern humans stopped using their emotions for what they were made for? If society were a person, it would be saying, 'It's not about you, it's about me.'

Like most psychologists, I learn a lot from my clients. Obviously, each individual story provides me with a rich insight into people's worlds and what's going on behind closed doors: how they feel, how they think and how they behave as a result. By listening to thousands of stories, psychologists can sense patterns in the way people react to certain problems, events, situations, issues and social phenomena in the world. As someone who is privileged to talk to people at their most vulnerable, I'm watching the human psyche respond to the world in real time. And even though clients present with their own individual stories, the themes of their distress are often remarkably similar.

I've had clients who are leaders of organisations and managers of huge teams who are chronically stressed, existing on little sleep and under immense pressure, trying desperately to find some sense of personal and professional balance. I've had employees feeling too psychologically unsafe to let their bosses know they have anxiety and can't come to work today, for fear of being fired. I've had business owners ready to give up on their dreams after watching other business owners spruik their (exaggerated) successes in their marketing campaigns and wondering why everyone else has a successful business but them. I've had entrepreneurs who have been coached to breaking point, being told that they need to hustle constantly, ditch their values and sell their soul for success. After all, success and earning tonnes of money is what really matters ... *right*?

I've had young people comparing their life to their social media connections' perfect highlight reels, wondering why everyone's life looks way better than theirs. I've had tech-addicted youth with disrupted circadian rhythms who feel anxious and depressed, are low in vitamin D and are scared to go outside.

I've had young parents who are struggling financially, grappling with the thought of going back to work when they deeply want to spend more time with their young children. I've had middle-aged clients who are part of the 'sandwich generation' – still working every day, looking after their children at home while also trying to care for their elderly parents.

I've had women working more hours to get the same money as men doing the same job. I've had women who are bombarded with media messages telling them they need to look, sound and be a certain way for society to value them. I've had men who appear angry but, once we go deeper, are actually anxious. They've been conditioned by society to keep their emotions inside of them. Because, after all, boys aren't supposed to cry. I've had gender-fluid clients who are grappling with a world that just doesn't understand so dismisses them, passing off their courage to own who they are as 'just a phase'.

I've had enthusiastic elderly clients who are full of ideas and energy, wanting to work but not able to get an interview. I've had people living alone in their homes, desperate to connect with the outside world but too uncomfortable to know where to start in a neighbourhood of people who don't chat much over the fence anymore.

I've had teachers who are expected to be 'on call' and available to their students' parents 24/7. I've had doctors who are supposed to be full of energy, empathy and clarity for their patients but who've been expected to work ridiculously long shifts, and won't ever complain for fear of being deemed mentally unfit for their role. I've got people with so many hats to wear – roles that involve multiple tasks and duties that probably would have been spread evenly across everyone in an entire village thousands of years ago.

Much of the distress felt by people is caused by the status quo. As Robert Iger, CEO of Walt Disney, said,

'The riskiest thing we can do is just maintain the status quo.' It's likely that many of the stressors and pressures we experience are a result of a culture that has totally mucked up its priorities and is operating from old limiting beliefs and outdated systems, which are long overdue for an upgrade. Many of us operate from a blueprint conditioned by the unconscious and subconscious messages from the society around us, all of which are contributing factors to our burnout.

Burnout rhetoric mostly revolves around our occupational settings, and rightly so. The places where many of us spend most of our time still have a long way to go. People who've burned out because of unrelenting occupational stress often talk about unmanageable workloads, unreasonable time pressures, unfair treatment by management and lack of support in the workplace. I've had clients give their soul to their workplace and get nothing in return.

We can sit here and blame society all we want, but it would be far more beneficial to continue these constructive discussions to help strategise a more humanistic way of working and start actioning the change. Our societies are made up of millions of people (going on eight billion on latest counts), so if we all raise our own consciousness about how we are feeling and why, and take our own steps to help ourselves feel better, the flow-on effect is going to be change. We're responsible for that. Change takes time, and small steps over time turn into a full journey. If we're all feeling and processing what's working and what isn't, and then taking steps to create our best selves and to reach our own potential, can you imagine the societal transformation that will be able to take place as a result?

We're never our best selves when we're burned out, and it's easier to blame others for the way things are (and sometimes it may be totally the fault of others). But things are the way they are (for now) and if we're going to fight the fight, and work to change that, well, we need our energy back to do so. Maybe if we can all stay clear of burnout, we can massively disrupt the status quo and change the world for the better.

PART 2

Beyond Burnout

Just Stop

'Doing nothing often leads to the very best of something.'

WINNIE THE POOH

ONE OF MY clients, Tom, was referred to me by his doctor for (what he thought was) depressive-like symptoms that had rendered him unable to work. He could not channel a molecule of energy to lift his head off the pillow in the morning, never mind drive himself to work. It was impossible for Tom to create the chain of psychological and physical events that were required to move himself to the place in which in whichhe had spent the past 20 years of his professional life. Even within his own home, he was moving at a glacial speed. For some, let's be honest, this is the speed at which they usually move, but it was the extreme opposite of how Tom normally operated. It was totally out of character for him.

What had initially started as a creeping feeling of unhappiness on the job, feeling a tad irritated at colleagues in the boardroom on occasion and a few sleepless nights here and there became a full-blown inability to solve any problems that were presented to him. He had zero capability to make a decision, even if it was about what to have for dinner, and an inability to get through any evening without at least one bottle of wine. On top of this, a general 'what is life all about' attitude had come over him and he was ready to pack in everything.

Not only was this problematic for Tom for obvious reasons, but it was even more troublesome because his workplace was his own business that he had built from scratch. He was a high-achieving, successful, well-known entrepreneur who had been excelling in his business and industry for a couple of decades. He had more than one hundred employees that he was responsible for, he had done so much for so long, and now ... he couldn't leave his house. He was so exhausted that he cancelled his psychologist appointments more than he attended them. Even showing up for that was too much to ask for on some days. This is burnout at its finest. No judgement.

The pressure that Tom was under (and had been under for a long time) was immense, and the flow-on effect of his now physical (and psychological) absence was massive. His staff didn't know what was going on and it was hard for him to tell them, given he didn't know what was going on either. All Tom knew was that he couldn't go to work and he didn't have the capability to pull himself out of whatever was going on for him. (Yet.)

The advice I gave to Tom, and that I give to anyone else who has reached the point of burnout, was to ... wait for it ... *stop*. Put down the tools, ring in sick, don't go to work and cancel all the activities and commitments that are written in your diary. Have time off, take sick leave, eat into your annual or long-service leave. Hell ... if you don't have any leave try to take leave without pay. You need to stop. Then, you need to rest; lay on the couch all day, sleep for hours and don't speak to anyone. Just give your brain and body the time it needs to get some molecules of energy back so that you can start thinking again.

One big problem is that people sabotage their ability to heal from burnout by judging themselves harshly for a) burning out in the first place; b) not being able to see it coming; c) not getting over it quickly enough; and d) caring far too much about the judgement they think others will place on them. Stopping, for many people, can be uncomfortable, if not impossible, eliciting a suite of emotions that can feel even worse than the initial emotions that led to burnout in the first place. So be mindful of any emotions such as guilt and shame. It's crucial in the burnout and recovery phase that we remove all self-judgement and move to a place of self-compassion.

However uncomfortable stopping is, it's imperative to push through the initial discomfort as much as you can. If a doctor or psychologist has not recommended it already (most of them are likely to), act as if one of us has written a pharmaceutical script with the word 'stop' on it. If you don't have your mental and physical health, it's impossible to heal.

Of course, stopping doesn't always have to mean sleeping and lying down (although it may initially). When some molecules of energy start creeping back in, stopping can still mean doing something – it just means stopping those things that were draining. As part of an intentional recovery process, think of activities that you know recharge, relax and refill your energy resources. Cooking, painting, reading, gardening, talking with friends or even doing a bit of physical exercise may help.

Once you get a taste of stopping and you're feeling more energised, you will start to realise the mental and physical benefits that stopping has for you. This realisation needs to flow on to making sure that breaks are part of everyday life going forward, no matter how busy you become. Research has shown that as little as ten minutes can give us the pick-me-up we need to reset. Known as micro-breaks, these are usually informal, unscheduled, non-structured moments that are used to re-energise us. A recent research review on micro-breaks showed that those who took them had about 60 per cent better odds of feeling energetic.[10] Reaping the benefits of a small pause involves listening to yourself throughout the day and checking in for any fatigue; and, if you do notice any, consciously taking a break and choosing another activity that is quite different to what you were doing. For example, if you've been sitting in an office, this could mean moving away from the computer and walking around outside. If your work involves physical exertion, such as a bricklaying, your micro-break needs to be non-physical.

While we're in the thickness of the burnout fog, we're often so quick to blame ourselves for not being able to cope well or keep up that we don't have the psychological capacity nor the energy to realise that other people in our lives could have been creating some of the feelings of distress we've been experiencing. That's why it's imperative that, in the stopping phase, we remove ourselves from certain people for a period of time – just while we are healing from burnout. It doesn't have to be a forever removal; it means taking time out, a pause in contact or a small break away from anyone who doesn't make us feel at peace.

When I was a kid and we wanted to a have a break from a game in the school playground, we'd yell, 'Barleese!' When I yell that to my kids now when we're mucking around, it means nothing, but back in the 80s in Australia, this was a very clear message to other people not to engage with us while we had a break from the game. It meant 'safe', 'stop' or 'pause', and with no questions asked, other kids always obeyed and just left us alone. (For a bit, anyways.) Burnout recovery needs a 'Barleese' of sorts with other people; it might be a short one, or a longer one. Whatever the length, it needs to be communicated to other people in your life, whether you know them personally or professionally.

The stopping phase doesn't have to mean a full quitting of anything – whether it's work, romance, a friendship, a business or a hobby – which is what many of my clients do in their heightened state of stress. Often, they feel quitting is their only option. It could be putting the brakes on a relationship like my client John had to do. John was a burned-out pharmacy owner. Unrelenting pandemic stress, no holidays for two years, endless staffing issues and a void of family time had rendered him completely psychologically and physically wiped out. And John, doing what many people do in these situations when they've become a workaholic – exhausted beyond repair and in endless emotional turmoil – began having an affair. The extra stress created by his questionable decisions caused John to become even more burned out. Part of his burnout recovery, right at the beginning of our work together, was to pause the relationship with this new lady. The affair was complicating everything and causing him more guilt and inner turmoil (as affairs, in their nature, don't tend to be public declarations) than it was bringing him pleasure.

Others I've worked with have had a break from work and all the people who come with it. Some have decided to work solely from home and only communicate with one designated (non-stressful) person who becomes the conduit for all others. Some people have stated to friends that they are not going out to any parties or events for a month and they will be in contact again soon. I've had mums who have said 'no' to play dates hosted at their houses. Other clients have put some boundaries in place with their in-laws during the festive season. And if we're not feeling the pull to be around certain people when we feel like this, then it might be a sign to pull back on our connection with them in the future.

All of us know someone who makes us feel happier simply by being around them, or someone who makes us feel at peace, at ease and calm. These people need to be kept around us when we're burned out. Some people are beacons of helpfulness when it comes to mental health, whereas others are not so much. We may need a break from people who have high expectations, demand too much of us, control us too much, judge us or who we can't be our true self around – at least until we are back on track and thinking clearly again about the world around us. Then we will have more clarity around how to navigate these types of people.

While recovering from a bout of burnout, we need to stop and simplify our life for a while. We'd do this if we had gastro, a virus or any other debilitating physical health condition, and we've got to do it with burnout. Without breaks to just stop, we're not giving ourselves the time we need to re-energise. Saying 'Barleese' regularly is crucial, not only for recovery but to optimise our performance in life.

Considerations

Do I want a break?

What would this look like?

Do I need to stop all my roles, or just some of them?

Do I need days, weeks or months off? How can I make this happen?

Who do I need to talk to about this?

Do I have rest breaks in my schedule?

Do I need to do less or more of something?

Do I need to set some time to rest, recharge and relax during my days going forward?

When can I do this? What days? What times?

What micro-break activities could I do in these moments?

What recovery activities can I incorporate into my weekly or monthly schedule?

Are there certain people in my life I need to take some time off from?

How could stopping more prevent burnout?

Challenge

Break Day

Try taking a day off completely and have nothing planned for a day. Tell those people close to you that you won't be reachable that day. This means no alarm set in the morning, no appointments booked, no answering phone calls, no responding to text messages and certainly no managing your email load. Be off the grid, but in your own home. Just simply be guided by what you feel like doing that day without the hustle and bustle of your usual tasks, chores, roles and duties. The only stipulation is that you make sure you are relaxing and taking time to rejuvenate. Notice at the end of the day how you feel from having this day off.

Commitment

Going forward, I commit to these new rituals to encourage more stopping and rest...

Notes

Be Emotional

'Emotion can be the enemy, if you give into your emotion, you lose yourself. You must be at one with your emotions, because the body always follows the mind.'

BRUCE LEE

WHEN MY DAUGHTER, Lali, was younger, she'd occasionally misbehave a little bit. It didn't happen very often, but when it did, we would always have a conversation about it. This involved taking her aside and having a chat about what happened, why the behaviour was inappropriate and what she could do next time she felt like that. You know, in other words ... next time you feel angry like that, perhaps punching your brother in the head isn't the best decision, so how about you do some deep breaths next time or 'use your words' a bit more in expressing how you're feeling?

These little chats always worked reasonably well, but what amused me the most was Lali's final statement at the end of these conversations. Whenever we finished up, I'd always ask her if she wanted to say anything else about it, and she'd say 'yes', and then respond with the most profound statement to wrap up what was probably, from her point of view, a rather uncomfortable conversation. With her eyes rolling upwards she would say, 'I think I need to go put on a dress.' Then, off she'd go and put one on. End of conversation. Other times, she'd rush off to put on a tiara, find her toy sheep or even just grab a random bowl from the kitchen to put a hair clip in (as toddlers do).

If only all of us could change how we feel in uncomfortable moments by simply putting on a dress or grabbing a bowl from the kitchen. In the inevitable event that you feel negative emotions again in the future (and when I say inevitable, I mean that you will), you need to know what to do with them. As they happen, too, not ten years later (or, in the case of some of my clients, 50 years later). Learning to be emotionally agile is an important tool for all of us, and if you get into the groove of it, it will literally change your life.

Feeling emotions is something that many of us don't tend to do that well. Nor do we express them that well. In today's busy world, we don't often slow down enough to notice the subtleties in our emotional changes. Instead, we succumb to their build-up, eventually becoming driven by them in such a way that it can makes things worse. If you've ever screamed at someone while driving or avoided someone because you've felt so ashamed, you'll know what I'm talking about. We're emotionally driven creatures us human beings, and it was necessary for us to feel extreme emotions at times for survival. But life is different now, and a greater understanding of our emotions and the complexities of life that could be causing them (apart from predators) is necessary for us to shift how we feel.

Emotional agility involves being psychologically flexible with our feelings and thoughts to respond appropriately to situations as they arise. Rather than being emotionally driven and not responding in an ideal way in the situation, it's about being able to feel, think, observe and manage the way we feel. It's more of a 'go with the flow' way of dealing with emotions – allowing them to be felt, but slowing it down a little so that everything is considered and the most accurate thoughts and appropriate behaviours are chosen to respond optimally.

If you have felt 'triggered' before, you will know that sometimes emotions can consume us and lead us to behave in ways that are not ideal. The limbic system in the brain controls our emotional and behavioural responses we need for survival, so it will turn on those alarm bells if it's presented with sensory information that is similar to a situation that happened in the past that psychologically or physically hurt us. Again, like many of our natural responses, they were helpful 100,000 years ago – but they're not always helpful now, if someone triggers us around a boardroom table in the workplace. Punching people in the face just because we feel we should isn't going to go down well for anyone.

So, what kinds of emotions could we feel? If you ask most people what some of the more pleasant emotions are, they'd probably list a handful of familiar ones such as happiness, love, surprise, joy or contentment, along with some less common ones such as excitement, gratitude, pride and awe. These positive emotions make us feel good and are information to the brain that all is well in our environment.

The emotions that we perceive as negative, such as anger, stress, fear, guilt and shame, are equally as important. Society still shuns some of these emotions, but all of them are valid and extremely valuable. Whether it's loneliness, emptiness, frustration, regret or misery, these emotions are telling us about our place in the context of our life, and that we might need to change something.

Shame, for example, is a powerful negative emotion. It resides deep down, often not emerging at all consciously during one's lifetime but nevertheless affecting the person who is holding on to it. If you've ever read any of author and researcher Brené Brown's work on shame, you will know the life-changing transformations that happen for people who start being open about their shame stories, and the soul destruction that happens when shame stories remain within. The fact that Brown's books are global bestsellers, and her vulnerability talk is one of the most watched inspirational TED Talks of all time, shows how much it resonates with her fellow human beings. Shame resides in many of us, and most of us have locked it away and thrown away the key.

Anger is another important emotion, yet one that society shuns and therefore we suppress. The suppressed emotion inevitably bubbles up to the surface and is expressed often with uncontrollable force. This makes things worse for the person feeling it, and the people around them.

The emotions that are elicited on the journey that leads to burnout are powerful pieces of information that are informing our brain as to what's working for us, what's not working for us and what needs to be adjusted in our life. Those emotions need to be felt, processed and analysed a little. Then, we do something to change the situation through our behaviours and actions to help shift those emotions. We could learn to observe the thoughts that we have about the situation and see if we can change those. Or, we change the way we feel and shift the emotion by doing things we know elicit a positive emotion in us. For example, going for a walk around the block after a heated discussion (a tried-and-true tactic, if ever there was one).

Going forward, noticing your emotions and feeling them accordingly is a must. Use them as a powerful guide in how to navigate the world in which you exist. They will help you understand what is working for you and what is not, and help you choose what direction is best for you.

Considerations

What emotions am I feeling now? Why do I feel like that?

What emotions have I felt today? Why could I be feeling like that?

What emotions do I tend to feel the most?

Has anyone given me feedback about my emotions?

Do I identify with being a certain type of emotion (e.g. an angry person)?

Do I feel certain emotions at certain times, in particular situations or around particular people?

What could these emotions be telling me?

Am I an emotionally driven person?

Are there any emotions I would like to feel more of?

How could being more emotional prevent burnout?

Challenge

Emotional Curiosity

Next time you feel a certain emotion within you, pause for a moment and be curious about it. Ask yourself what the feeling is and why you might be feeling like that. Then, ask yourself what powerful piece of information your brain is trying to tell you. Sense whether it is best in the moment to work on problem-solving what's going on, whether it's better to try to commit to thinking about this differently or whether it's more about trying to shift how you feel right now. Slow down the process and slip into a more inquisitive state before you act. Then, make a choice about what is best for you in the present moment. Repeat this across the course of the month and notice how you feel as a result.

Commitment

Going forward, I commit to these new rituals to help support my emotions...

Notes

Attend to the Signals

'No one can listen to your body for you ... to grow and heal, you have to take responsibility for listening to it yourself.'

JON KABAT-ZINN

ONE OF MY favourite movies from my childhood was *The Money Pit*. It starred a very youthful-looking Tom Hanks and centred around Walter and Anna, a couple who bought a magnificent turn-of-the-century mansion at a bargain price. Little did they know that the house of their dreams was a renovator's delight on steroids. Watching Walter and Anna move through the range of emotions, to the point they nearly descend into madness, is next-level entertainment. From romanticised excitement when they first move in, to confusion when little things start going wrong, to sheer terror as the dilapidated house literally falls apart before their eyes.

Apart from the hilarity that ensues throughout the film, there is one particular scene that, in my honest opinion, is one of the best movie scenes of all time. It's one that I'm sure would resonate with many of us who've got to breaking point after a string of life stressors. After an exhausting day of fixing up everything that was falling apart – the front door falling off its hinges, bee infestations in the garden, electrical wirings in the wall catching fire and blowing up every kitchen appliance, rain pouring in through holes in the roof and the whole grand Victorian staircase crumbling and falling to the floor (you know, usual reno stuff), the couple attempts to take a relaxing bath. After carrying several buckets of warm water to the bathroom on a ladder (because no staircase anymore ... of course), Walter exhaustedly pours the last of the buckets into the extravagant clawfoot bath. The bath then falls through the floor and smashes to smithereens on the floor of the first storey below (google it). As funny as this bit is, it's the 'crazy laugh' from Walter that makes the scene: an enormously loud, from-the-belly, scratch-your-throat, spit-flying-everywhere crazy laugh. His response, looking down through the hole in the floor to his smashed bath below, is the laugh you give, that we all give, when you are dealt the last straw. You know that laugh isn't about anything being funny; it's the laugh of sheer madness when nothing at all is going right, and you don't know what the hell you've done to deserve this laugh. The crazy laugh. You know the one.

This is what an emotional build-up can lead to. A slow build-up might happen when you just keep going, and then just one more thing goes badly or one more person says the wrong thing and then BOOM, you lose it. Crazy laugh (or something even worse). It's like you're way past the point of a polite display of emotion by then, and with that kind of emotional build-up, the outburst would not have done what you're feeling any justice. A build-up of negative emotion can lead to an explosion of emotion that is often carried out in a rather socially unacceptable and inappropriate manner.

We want to avoid the build-up of emotions. We want to be able to notice the signals that our brain and body are giving us as we go along so that we can stop and do something about them. Those signals are valuable little alarm bells that are telling us about something in our environment that we need to pay attention to. They give us the information we need to move away from something to keep us safe. And, on the flip side, once we've recovered from burnout we're more tuned in, and much more aware of the signals whispering to us about where the good stuff is, where the opportunities ahead lie and what the right directions are that we need to take to create a more aligned life.

Often when people see their doctor or mental health professional for burnout, they are at breaking point. They don't know what they are feeling or why there are feeling like that. They are so engulfed in burnout that it's too hard for them to separate themselves from it to understand it all. The signs and symptoms had likely been there a while – maybe days, weeks, months or even years – but they have now accumulated to a point where mental, physical, emotional and spiritual exhaustion have taken over. But the key here is that the warning signals would have been there all along, when the brain and the body had determined it was getting a little too much and was trying to communicate that.

As we've established, there are many different types of emotions that have an influence on how we live and interact with the world around us. Each one of them needs to be felt and then expressed in the right way – this is emotional agility. Happiness, for example, is expressed through facial expressions such as open eyes and smiling, body language such as an open and relaxed stance and a tone of voice that's energised and upbeat. We can *feel* happy, and people can see that we're happy.

When our brain is perceiving things in our environment that it deems are not okay for us, it will likely be sending mind and body signals warning us that something isn't quite right, and we need to adjust something accordingly. Part of the secret to being emotionally agile is noticing the signals, and then using them as the powerful red flags that they are.

So, what are these warning signals for burnout? Obviously, there are warnings that could communicate that we're stressed, but as we've established, there are some other emotions involved in becoming burned out. For me, the early warning signals when everything is becoming too much are my back becoming sore and my neck becoming tense. I also tend to become a little accident-prone – slicing my fingers when cooking, banging my arms on doorknobs, dropping dishes and tripping over all over the place. It's body fatigue that seems to get me more than anything. I tend to be particularly susceptible to falling up my stairs (particularly when I'm wearing those wide-legged pyjama bottoms – they are risky attire when you're exhausted). I know that, in the past, I've been so busy that negative emotions stopped trying to warn me and instead they talked through my body. So, when I notice another glass shattering or another rolled ankle, I start thinking about what needs to be actioned. If you have read any of author Louise Hay's work on how unexpressed emotions manifest themselves through the body, you will see what havoc they can cause. Remember my frozen shoulder from a few years back? It was likely to have been unexpressed overwhelm and a feeling like the world was on my shoulders (of course).

For some people, the signals can be the feelings themselves – perhaps we're feeling stressed, anxious, angry or endlessly frustrated. Maybe we are nervous, fearful or scared. Maybe we feel a sense of helplessness or of being trapped. Perhaps we just feel low or dissatisfied with life. Perhaps we're worrying about things in the future or ruminating about things in the past and find it hard to concentrate on the present moment. Maybe it's hard to concentrate at work and we keep making mistakes. Maybe we keep focusing on our problems and can't get them out of our mind. Maybe more people than usual are making us angry and we're getting into more arguments. Maybe we just can't stand people anymore. Maybe we're procrastinating and just can't do the work around the house that really is the priority.

Perhaps it's our body signalling something to us. Maybe we have a sinus infection that won't clear up, no matter how many antibiotic courses we take. Maybe the headaches have ramped up more than usual. Maybe we can't stop eating and we've been scavenging the kitchen for anything sweet. Maybe it's become impossible to not have an additional glass of wine. Maybe we're not sleeping, and we keep waking on the hour, every hour. Maybe we are sleeping, but we're just so, so tired.

There will be little signals every day that are telling us about aspects of our life that need to be adjusted. We need to notice these and start asking ourselves what they are all about. We must be inquisitive and curious as to what our minds and bodies are signalling to us, and identify why this could be the case. Then, we can start controlling our behaviours to steer ourselves back to a calmer state that our body loves to operate in.

Philosopher Socrates once said, 'Know thyself.' So, let's make sure that we do know ourselves so we can choose what to do next.

Considerations

What are the warning signals that my mind is giving me that are telling me something is not right?

Do these warning signals happen at particular times?

Do these warning signals happen in certain situations?

Do these warning signals happen in the presence of specific people?

Is there a theme to when these signals occur, or is it just a sign of overwhelm in general?

Do I know what to do when these signals are alerting me?

How could knowing what my signals are prevent burnout?

Challenge

Reflective Journalling

The next time you find your body and mind are whispering to you in the form of a warning signal, journal about exactly what is happening in your surroundings at the time. Write down what time it happened, where you were, who you were with, how you interpreted what was going on and, of course, how you were feeling at the time. Also, make notes of what else is going on in your life around that moment. Try to repeat this for at least a month. Reflective journalling is a powerful tool to help monitor what's going on your life and help analyse why something is impacting you. It gives you the information you need to decide what you need to do next. Spend some time doing this at the end of each day, and notice how you feel as a result of this practice.

Commitment

Going forward, I commit to these new rituals to help better understand how my mind and body are communicating with me...

Notes

Control Your Thoughts

'If you can change your mind,
you can change your life.'

WILLIAM JAMES

AS I MENTIONED earlier, a feeling is an experience of emotion, and our feelings are largely responsible for our entire experience of life. We can be driven by how we feel, but the way we *think* can change the way we feel. What's on our mind, and what we do with those thoughts, also affects how we feel. This is kind of cool when you consider the role this can play in healing from burnout and keeping it at bay in the future.

When we are feeling a certain way, it's important that we are curious as to why we feel like that. This special skill is something we have that separates us humans from lower-order animals, such as our cat. If our cat is feeling scared, it doesn't think about why, it just feels scared and then its behaviour reflects that. It also doesn't spend any time after the fact reflecting on why it overreacted earlier that day. It doesn't discuss with its neighbourhood cat friends the happenings of that stressful morning and it doesn't seek to do any personal development to grow from the experience (although we can hire a cat behaviourist for that I'm sure). We are not our family cat. We can feel an emotion, and then think about it before we behave. There is a space in between feeling and behaviour, and it is important that we use that space wisely.

When you are feeling stressed, try to analyse it a bit. Not six-years-plus university-trained analyse, but just think a little bit more about why you might be feeling stressed. Why is your brain turning this emotion on? And given the feeling is your experience of what is going on in your world, can you think more about it and see if you can do something to help yourself? Your brain is powerful and is taking in everything from your external and internal world and creating emotions in response to that. No matter where the original information came from (the outside world or your internal world), it will sit in your brain to be processed for a while – so it pays to tune into that. You have more time to think than you think (that's a lot of thinking!). In fact, us psychologists call this 'metacognition', which means thinking about thinking.

It's important for us to observe the thoughts in our mind. Perhaps those thoughts are about a particular area of our life. Maybe the thoughts are about our work. Specifically, they could be about a looming deadline we don't think we can meet, constant changes we can't seem to keep up with, unrelenting pressure regarding a particular project, bullying by a member of our team or a highly narcissistic boss who keeps badgering us on the weekend. Or maybe the thoughts revolve around the fact that we don't like our job anymore but we just don't know what to do next.

Maybe the thoughts are about our relationship. Maybe we've been having difficulties with our partner. Maybe we are finding that we haven't had enough time to spend with them lately. Maybe it's because we're not in a relationship, because we have recently separated, or maybe we can't find 'the one' and we don't want to spend any more evenings with mismatched Tinder dates and stupid conversations that go nowhere. Maybe the thoughts revolve around happenings in our home, or with our family. Maybe we have elderly parents. Maybe we have financial difficulties. Maybe we have constant thoughts about someone we are still grieving for, and we can't seem to get them out of our mind.

Maybe our thoughts expand to the world environment, and we're absorbing the goings-on across the globe, reading about crisis after crisis reported in the media. Perhaps because we're a caring, empathic citizen, we're constantly wondering what the world is coming to, and it sits in our mind every single day. Maybe our thoughts are about all of it. Maybe our thoughts are about something else.

Whatever is on our mind, though, it's important to know what it is. Observe it. Then, we can work with what it is trying to communicate to us. When we notice a thought, it's helpful to ask ourselves: is this something I can do something about? Or can I do something to change the way I feel right now? Whatever we do, we're not meant to ignore the thoughts nor bottle them up.

As we've established, there is always a lot going on in our external world that our brain is constantly interacting with. But in some cases, we can be feeling a certain way because we are thinking in an unhelpful way that is creating more stress than necessary. Our emotions are responding to the outside world, but also to the way we think internally (which can often be distorted). Most of us go about thinking what we think, without thinking anything of it and distressing ourselves in the process (so that's a lot of thinking ... again!).

As conscious beings, we are always interpreting the world around us, trying to make sense of what is happening. But what if we're getting our thinking wrong, and then going about our day being wrong about certain things? Chances are this is happening to all of us to some degree, which is causing us unnecessary stress and anxiety. If you think of how many thoughts weave across your mind each day (a 2020 study reported that people typically have about 6000 thoughts per day), we don't want to be making too many mistakes in thinking, and feeling rotten as a result![11]

Unhelpful thinking styles are known as cognitive

distortions. If you're thinking that you don't have any and that your thought processes are totally on point, literally, think again. It's likely that all of us have distorted thinking. Our ancestors would have had very efficient ways of thinking thousands of years ago, and these ways of thinking would have served them very well at the time. In fact, our thinking styles would have been 'helpful' thinking styles that back then. Those Homo sapiens that didn't jump to conclusions or catastrophise would have been killed off a long time ago. We all come from a long line of anxious Homo sapiens who, because of their cautionary nature and what we often see as 'silly' ways of thinking, kept their pack safe by always predicting the worst. But alas, like lots of things in the modern world, old ways of thinking don't always serve us well now. They can make us downright miserable and burned out.

One of my clients, Tim, was an excessive personaliser. Everything that seemingly didn't work out in his life was interpreted (by himself) as his fault, and his fault only. He saw himself as the sole reason as to why nothing went right, ever. This way of thinking left him feeling hopeless, worthless and with no oomph at all to put effort into trying to create a better life because, after all, what's the point? He'd just wreck it. This was not true from my angle but it was Tim's strong belief; he'd thought these thoughts repeatedly throughout his life.

While all of us personalise things to some extent (as it's wired into us), there are many people who do it more than others, which is something that possibly started out in their childhood. Constantly blaming ourselves for things that happen to us can decrease our confidence to try new things (and gain more confidence). It also moves us out of problem-solving mode in which we could make things better. Working with Tim involved helping him to cognitively reinterpret things that happened to him (in the past, and in the present) so that he could see alternative explanations as to why these things happened. He wasn't to blame for every little thing that went wrong and, slowly over time, he could see that. He could come up with a range of reasons why situations happened, why people said certain things and, most of all, why women didn't get back to him after a first date (this was a common problem, I'm telling you) that had nothing to do with him. He gained a more balanced perspective on life, and his place in it. Turns out, the world wasn't against him. One of my greatest enjoyments as a psychologist is seeing a client move from being self-blaming internally to self-confident (and, in Tim's case, a little feisty too!).

There are quite a few unhelpful thinking styles or cognitive distortions that can lead to an unnecessary emotional build-up, and it's important that we check in with ourselves regularly to see if we're using any of them

– particularly when the emotion is negative, and we can't shift the thought.

Perhaps you are prone to catastrophising and blowing things out of proportion, viewing every problem as the end of the world. If you've ever found a lump on your body or a strange freckle and started picking out the music for your funeral straight away, you know what I'm talking about. Perhaps we partake in 'magnification and minimisation' a little too much, where we inflate things that are insignificant and minimise things that should be bigger. We might find ourselves honing in on the one bad thing that happened on a day when a hundred good things happened, too, which we totally missed. Notice what you talk about with people in your household in the evening – is it a balanced account of the good and the bad?

Maybe our thoughts are too 'all or nothing' or 'black and white', without us entertaining the grey area. Anyone who's made a mistake at work and concluded that they are a complete failure and might lose their job will resonate here. Perhaps everything needs to be perfect at home, and if it isn't it's the end of the world, causing constant irritation. Yes, I know, it's annoying when people throw our fluffy cushions everywhere, but it doesn't mean the world is going to end, even if in our mind it feels that way. These unhelpful ways of thinking cause unhelpful emotional distress.

Another cognitive thinking style that probably would have served us very well as a cave person is 'mind-reading'. Back in the day when we encountered people who were not speaking the same language as us, we would take what we did know (in a very unconsciously biased way, of course), read their minds and then act accordingly. We didn't stop, have a chat or try to figure out and understand what they were saying or meaning. They could have been dangerous, of course, so it was better to just presume the worst. Fast forward to today, and we do the same thing. Keep an eye out for the conclusions you jump to when people haven't answered a text message, when the barista doesn't laugh at your joke when you're ordering your morning latte, or when you're left on 'unopened' on WhatsApp. As a professional speaker, I'm particularly susceptible to my audience members' body language. There's nothing like a side-eye or a yawn to spook a public speaker.

Us modern humans are also quite accomplished at 'fortune telling'. If we've ever had a difficult encounter with someone (or even heard that they are difficult), it's automatic that we will predict that in the future, when we encounter the same person, they will be difficult. Our brain holds on to a lot of important information about our experiences, so it will predict what could happen next given the information it has (and, yes, it always prepares for the worst). We make assumptions about people, events and situations before they have occurred – and likely worry unnecessarily about them or even stop ourselves from moving forward in directions that are necessary for us. The future doesn't exist yet, so we need to keep ourselves open to the endless possibilities. Difficult people can be really be nice at times!

Thoughts are not facts. Just because we think it, doesn't mean it's true. We need to question our thoughts and check whether they are helpful and worth hanging on to. Of course, some thoughts are worth ditching completely. Some thoughts are an enormous waste of time and are taking up space in our mind that could otherwise be used to store more important information (such as exciting goals we have, brilliant ideas we want to actualise, new books we want to read, chocolate, cute dogs, Ryan Gosling, etc. – or maybe that's just me).

Learning to let go of some thoughts is a powerful technique that can also help us shift unhelpful, unneeded and unwanted thoughts out of our mind. It involves noticing our thought, deciding whether it is worthy of staying and, if not, consciously letting it go. This can mean watching it in our mind as it floats off into the sky, or we can visually put it on a leaf and watch it float down a stream. Or you can do what I do and state 'not thinking about this' and then purposefully distract yourself with something else – TV, a book, cooking or 80s love songs (again, that's just me).

We can also challenge our pesky negative thoughts. Think of a friend who is a very helpful (and considerate) devil's advocate to what you say. Or imagine you're a therapist. Gosh, even pretend I'm talking to you (which I kind of am) and challenge those thoughts that won't shift. It's important to ask yourself these questions: is this a fact? Is there any evidence to support what I'm thinking here? What is the evidence that is suggesting what I'm thinking to be true? Then, think about alternative thoughts on purpose. Consider arguing with yourself a little. Is there any evidence against the thoughts I'm thinking? What are the alternate perspectives here? Examine the evidence and see if there are alternative explanations for your thoughts, and perhaps add a bit of evidence that your thoughts are wrong (just like if you were in a debate on the side you don't agree with). Take some time to come up with some proof that perhaps your thoughts are wrong, and you've been unnecessarily distressing yourself as a result.

Remember, it's not the stress that's the problem, it's what we do with it that matters the most. Sometimes we are accidentally stressing ourselves out by engaging in thinking that makes things a whole lot worse. If we looked at our thinking a little more, analysed it a tad and changed it a bit, we would change the way we feel, steering us back to a healthier way of thinking and away from burnout.

Always remember that we have the power to change our thoughts. Initially, our brain will try to control us, but we can always take back the reins and bring it back under our control. Also remember we're not cats (obviously), so that space between feeling and behaviour is ours for the taking.

Considerations

What's on my mind?

Am I experiencing any recurring thoughts?

Do these thoughts happen at particular times?

Do these thoughts happen in certain situations?

Do these thoughts happen in the presence of specific people?

Do these thoughts happen more when I'm alone?

Are there particular themes or topics to my thoughts?

Am I engaging in any unhelpful thinking styles, such as catastrophising, magnifying/minimising, personalising, all-or-nothing thinking, mind-reading or fortune telling?

Could I reinterpret my thoughts to a more realistic way of thinking?

How could controlling my thoughts prevent burnout?

Challenge

Friendly Self-Talk

Next time you feel like your thoughts are a little out of control, try talking to yourself like you would one of your friends. We are always 'peak sage' when we are giving advice to other people and full of the wisest advice, so try to do that in the form of self-talk. Next time an unhelpful thought crops up that is causing you distress, point out to yourself that it might be an unhelpful thinking style and give yourself some alternative explanations around what you are thinking about. Compassionately disagree with yourself, just like a friend would, and offer yourself other reasons and considerations to keep in mind, other than what the dominant thought is. This gives you a chance to create some new perspectives in your mind and, hopefully, alleviate any unnecessary distress – just like our mates do for us when we catch up with them.

Commitment

Going forward,
I commit to these
new rituals to
develop a greater
understanding of
my relationship
with my thoughts...

Notes

Learn to Be

'Almost everything will work again if you unplug it for a few minutes, including you.'

ANNE LAMOTT

THERE'S A SAYING by the Dalai Lama that goes, 'We are human beings not human doings.' While the sentiment is certainly true, and it wouldn't be wise to debate the Dalai Lama's teachings, if we are to apply this realistically to our lives we need both. We need to find a sweet spot between being and doing so we can achieve what we want in life.

Let's face it, those of us who are prone to burning out spend a lot of time being busy. We're continuously on the go with the multiple hats we wear and have likely been operating like this for a long time. We generally spend more time *doing* than we do *being*, and as a result are not mindfully engaged in whatever activity we are doing. It's like we're living two lives: our body in the present moment, and our mind somewhere else. If you've ever driven down the freeway and missed your exit without even noticing, this will resonate. Or maybe you left the hair straightener off but thought you'd left it on, and didn't remember that you'd turned it off until an hour later while you're at work (or maybe that's just me). This is because our body was there at the time, as well as our brain on some level, but our mind was elsewhere. We were not 100 per cent being in the moment, and this can be problematic.

In the contemporary world, where we are being conditioned by external forces to focus on doing, doing, doing with a mind that rarely stops to spend time in the present moment, incorporating time to just be needs to be given more credence. Without those moments to be present, process the day, reflect and just think, we can find ourselves on an unhealthy trajectory towards burning out. That's why learning to just be, even if only for a few minutes, needs to be ritualised into our schedule.

Contrary to what many people think, we don't have to move to an ashram to find time to be. Nor do we have to fly overseas to a treetop health retreat or head out hiking in the desert. While all of these 'being' adventures sound revitalising and would likely do the trick, these bigger quests for peace and calm can be quite unrealistic for many of us (like, who is gonna look after the kids, water the plants, put the cat out ... all the things?). That's why, in keeping burnout at bay, we've got to think a little more realistically and ask ourselves how, on an average day, we can just ... be?

But what does it take to simply *be*? It involves being proactive in organising some time to bring ourselves back to the present moment. It's about using little touch points throughout the day to bring ourselves back into physical and psychological alignment. We all can do this, but I think many of us have forgotten how to do it (or be it, for that matter).

Meditation and mindfulness activities are very helpful here. Perhaps we've dabbled in them a bit and given up, rendering it impossible with a mind that won't keep quiet. Or maybe we've found the activity of sitting on a cushion cross-legged while humming positively silly. Perhaps we can't even sit on a cushion cross-legged. Meditation is certainly something I recommend to all my clients, even when I'm met with rolling eyes. For those who are not au fait with meditation, it can feel like we need to find a big chunk of time to do it or even need years of training to be able to benefit from it, so people tend block the idea of it way too quickly. It can also sound a bit too 'woo woo' to some and this frightens them off, so I always tread carefully when I raise the idea of meditation.

Meditation is a practice where we focus our mind on a particular thought, activity or even object. By doing this, we can train our attention and awareness to this one thing, which allows our body and mind to align to the present moment and calm our nervous system. One of the many wonderful aspects of meditation is that the benefits can come from any of the many styles of it – whether it's for ten minutes or an hour, whether it's done quietly or with chanting, whether we're being led by someone or doing it alone and whether it involves music or silence. Many people starting out practise for a short amount of time and usually like to be led by someone else talking them through the steps to becoming calmer. A lot of my clients (many of whom work a ridiculous number of hours a day) prefer to start their day with a 20-minute meditation as part of their morning ritual – before the demands of their day are imposed on them. By popping on some earphones and listening to their favourite meditation app, they can take control of their day before it even begins.

Mindfulness is like meditation, in that it involves paying attention to the present moment with full awareness, but it is more about engaging in the sensory experience of attending to the now. In allowing our mind and body to be attentive to the moment, we are likely to become more in tune with ourselves, hear what our brain and body needs from us and be more accepting of our own thoughts and emotions. For some of my clients, this means taking themselves to a park at lunchtime and enjoying their sushi in peace away from their desk and interrupting colleagues. Others will take a moment in their car after dropping off the kids to school to close their eyes for ten minutes before charging off to their next commitment. Some will stop and purposefully engage in a mindfulness activity such as colouring in, jigsaw puzzles or painting to help recalibrate throughout the day.

'Being' might mean consciously engaging in the present moment with our tasks instead of the non-intentional multitasking that we're so used to. For example, when our partner gets home from work, we might stop cooking dinner and give them our full attention for ten minutes to chat about the day. It might mean turning off our phone during mealtimes so we're not interrupted by others while eating dinner with our family. Or it might mean being fully engaged with our kids at their after-school activities, watching them instead of using it as time to catch up on emails. Doing one thing mindfully at a time allows us the chance to be present, instead of engaging in the mind exhaustion of doing too many things at once.

Even just adjusting the way we breathe has the power to help us 'be'. When we're rushing through our day, our breathing often becomes shallow, which contributes to our fight, flight or freeze response being activated. Purposefully stopping throughout our day and calibrating our nervous system with some deep breathing can bring us back to a homeostatic state. Diaphragmatic (belly) breathing, which involves deep, slow inhales and exhales from our abdomen, has been shown to improve stress, anxiety and depressive symptoms.[12]

The changing or creating of any habit is often difficult,

particularly when we don't normally do it. But the more we practise being present and engaging fully in an activity with all our senses, the easier it is. Over time, it will likely become your new normal. You never know, you might enjoy the present. It's quite nice here.

Considerations

Do I feel disconnected from the moment throughout the day?

Are there particular times or situations where I feel less engaged?

Do I tend to drift off mentally when people are talking to me?

Have I had any feedback from people around me that I am not present at times?

Are there any activities that I enjoy doing where I feel fully present and in a flow state?

Could I incorporate more time in the day to engage in these activities?

Do I have small windows in the day where I can stop for a moment and 'be'?

Can I incorporate some new mindfulness or meditation activities into my schedule?

Can I engage in more hobbies and activities that I love?

When would be the best and most realistic time for me to do this?

How can learning to 'be' prevent burnout?

Challenge

Morning Ritual

It can sometimes be difficult to find a moment during the day to just be, particularly at the beginning of a 'being journey' – that's why starting the day with a morning ritual can work well. Set your alarm for 20 minutes before you usually do, before the hustle and bustle of your day. Get up and sit in a quiet area of your home (preferably don't even leave your bedroom), without checking your phone or turning on the TV or radio, and do 20 deep breaths to centre yourself. Focus solely on breathing in through your nose for five seconds and filling up your lungs, holding the breath for five seconds and then slowly breathing out of your mouth for five seconds. Repeat this, focusing on the direction of the airflow and centring yourself in the process. Notice how you feel afterwards.

Commitment

Going forward, I commit to these new rituals to help bring me into the present moment...

Notes

Check Your Childhood

'Children are like wet cement.
Whatever falls on them
makes an impression.'

DR HAIM GINOTT

HANNAH WAS A 28-year-old woman who started seeing me a few years ago. She was referred by her doctor with the presenting problems being depression and anxiety. At the beginning of our first session together she said, 'I think I want to leave my husband.' Hannah was an executive assistant who loved her job but had been on leave for a period while raising her two small children. Her husband had a busy management job and he worked full-time, often working late. Hannah was slowly trying to resume her career and was easing back into working part-time, but was becoming quite distressed at how difficult the juggle was.

Raising two small children under four, working three days a week, dropping the kids at day care, keeping a clean and functioning home, keeping the family fed and watered, driving the kids to their activities, being a happy and engaged wife, maintaining her own social life and having time to exercise was proving to be impossible. The pressure on Hannah was too much and she had been feeling constantly overwhelmed and not good enough.

In one of my early sessions with Hannah, we were discussing her anxiety and she mentioned the ebb-and-flow nature of the symptoms. She didn't feel anxious all the time, but there were certain moments or periods of time that she felt the symptoms escalate. Namely, in and around visits from her mother, with even a phone call being enough to set off a chain of anxious symptoms. As lovely and 'helpful' as Hannah consciously described her mother, there was obviously something about her presence or even having a phone conversation with her that was impacting Hannah.

Hannah had grown up in a house with two loving parents; her father worked full-time and her mother was a stay-at-home mum who looked after the children and kept a 'very clean' house. Memories of childhood, albeit full of love and care, were peppered with Mum becoming angry over toys being left out, crumbs dropped on the floor or anything being unkempt. Hannah recalls her childhood home as being immaculate, with the fragrance of bleach being the dominant scent. Hannah and her brother were expected not to make a mess and knew that anything they played with would need to be packed away immediately in the right spot. Otherwise ... big trouble.

These expectations were reasonably easy for Hannah to obey, and she learned very early on in her life to keep everything spotless in the home for Mum. She was a 'good girl' who was tidy and always helped her mum out. Even in her teenage years, when her mother was out with friends, Hannah would always make sure the dishes were done, the floor was swept and the counters were wiped so that Mum could walk in the house and be happy. Her tidiness, her thoughtfulness and her compliance kept Mum happy, and the house was kept peaceful.

As children, we are positively reinforced for certain behaviours and continue doing them when it's highly regarded by people in our context, meaning that we learn to repeat behaviours that work for others (and us at times). But we can also be negatively reinforced. This means that we can learn very early what behaviours we need to do to avoid adverse behaviour from those around us. In Hannah's case, she was conditioned to keep everything looking clean in her household growing up. Everything needed to be perfect. Otherwise, she had learned that Mum would be upset.

This conditioning flowed through Hannah's psyche, and this is how she continued to behave in adulthood. Having high standards was an admirable quality, and so was wanting everything to be perfect. This was manageable for a while in her early adulthood as a single woman, but almost impossible as a working mother of two.

Us adults all operate from a blueprint that was designed

when we were little. For Hannah, the blueprint of a perfect house and the 'be seen and not heard' parenting philosophy of the past didn't work for her consciously, but she was still distressed with it not being actualised in her home. The expectations that were placed on her were too high. It's almost impossible to have a career, look after and play games with our children, cook healthy meals every night, keep fit and healthy, spend time with our partner plus time on our own and meet all our needs in today's world. It's impossible for everything to be perfect. And even when it is, it will change a second later. Yet here we are, still operating like we did when we were growing up, fulfilling the same roles that we did in our childhood homes.

Of course, some of us have done some personal development since our childhood, but for the most part, we haven't because adulthood got in the way, and we just got busy. It's important to explore how we operated in our childhood and teenage years and how that made us the people we are now. Obviously, there are traumatic childhood experiences that can inflict wounds on a child and therefore the adult, but there are also seemingly insignificant roles and parts we played in our childhood that can still affect our adult psyche. Often, the way we are may have helped us in our childhood – helped us navigate our family system with all its glorious (and not-so-glorious) personalities – but it might not be helpful now as adults.

Looking back on our past, perhaps we were the eldest child who took care of everyone, so we still see that as our role now. Or maybe we were the baby of a large family who was taken care of by other people and we find it hard to do it alone now, so everything keeps piling up. Maybe we lived in a house where children were seen and not heard, so we struggle with speaking up at work. Perhaps a parent passed away when we were a child and we stepped up to be the caregiver and provider for everyone way too early, and now we just don't know how to not be that. Perhaps we had a parent who gave us heaps of attention when we did well at school and not as much attention otherwise, so we are constantly striving to achieve and don't know how to stop. Perhaps we were told 'boys don't cry', so we learned very early on to keep our feelings to ourselves. Perhaps we learned that the house needed to look perfect to be the best mum, so when it's not, we get terribly anxious.

Sometimes, the moments where we are 'triggered' can give us a little clue about circumstances that affected us in the past. For Hannah, this would have been toys all over the floor, a comment about a messy house from her husband or even just her mother calling. These triggers are something we need to be conscious of and, if we don't want to be reactive to them, we must explore ways of not letting them affect us.

Us psychologists often can't help but learn from others when we're working with our clients. While we're listening to thousands of human stories over the years, we can't help but reflect on our own. Between my own client work and my professional development, I'm continuing to learn about my own self to this day. Little light-bulb moments arise for me as well as my clients throughout our sessions as we work hard like detectives to uncover why we are the way we are. There's excitement in the aha moment that comes when the mystery is solved, and then the relief. Often, when the unconscious becomes conscious, we can embark on the journey of changing to something that works better for us. Some of the ways we unconsciously operated worked for us back then, but they might not be working for us now. And unfortunately, they could be impacting our wellbeing in the now or even contributing to a stress load we can't shift.

For Hannah, it was realising she needed to embrace imperfection. It was impossible for her to perform all of her roles at the standard she (or her inner child) was expecting. She needed to cut herself some slack and sit in the discomfort of her house being a little bit messy, of not always sitting down on the floor playing with her kids and of embracing takeaway food now and again. Her recovery also involved having a conversation with her hubby ... and her mother.

Pulling ourselves back from burnout involves having a little chat with our inner child, because the way we were raised may not be working for us anymore. Uncovering these patterns allows us the chance to change them. Often it's best to reach out to a mental health professional to help you reach deeper into your psyche and help you uncover and process these memories accordingly. With these insights, we can move towards something that is more aligned with how we want to live in the present and supports the way we want to feel.

Considerations

How would I describe my childhood?

Thinking back to my childhood, were there any significant events that happened?

What was my relationship like with my mother and father?

How did they interact with me? How did they communicate with me?

Were there any difficult things about my childhood? How was I disciplined? How did I feel when I was disciplined?

Do I remember any significant pressures or stressors?

Do I have any triggers from my childhood? If so, what are they?

Do I feel that my childhood experiences have influenced me as an adult?

How could acknowledging my childhood and all that I learned throughout that period help prevent burnout?

Challenge

Childhood Reflections

Close your eyes and think back to when you were ten years old, living at home with your caregivers. Walk around the home, into each room and notice what is going on in the environment. Use all your senses while you are walking around and take in what you see, what you hear and what you smell, and touch different objects as you walk throughout the home. Notice who is there. Notice what they are saying and what topics are being discussed. Notice the different roles everyone plays in the house and, most importantly, think about how you feel. Once you open your eyes and return to the present moment, think about how much of your childhood is recreated in some way in your present life, and whether it is negatively impacting your wellbeing. Is there anything you can change to ease the pressure?

Commitment

Going forward,
I commit to these
new rituals to
gain a greater
understanding
about the role my
childhood plays
in the present
moment...

Notes

Feed Your Soul

'In your soul are infinitely precious things that cannot be taken from you.'

OSCAR WILDE

A FEW YEARS back, I was working with a client called May. May had come to a presentation of mine called 'The Thriving Professional', which outlines the areas high-achieving professionals need to nurture on their path to success so that they can be mentally healthy *and* enjoy life. She reached out a few weeks later to see if I was taking on new clients.

May was a registrar doctor who was working long hours, feeling exhausted and under a lot of pressure so early on in her career. In the previous few months, she had found herself questioning whether being a doctor was the right profession for her. Apart from the heavy workload and occasional screaming consultant, she found it an all-consuming career which was affecting her personally. She didn't have a social life anymore and she didn't have a chance to engage in any of her other interests, such as cooking and fashion. She was judging herself harshly for considering quitting when she had spent so many years studying medicine. But the most fearful thing for May was her parents' judgement if she were to quit. In fact, she said they 'would kill her'. Not in a murder type of way, but in a bitterly disappointed and shame-inducing parent type of way – which, in many cultures, is even worse.

When I first met May, she looked like a walking piece of art. Wearing bright lipstick, colourful dresses and always with a perfectly matched flower looped into her hair, it was hard not to be blown away by her style. You didn't have to be Einstein (or Dolce & Gabbana) to know what she truly wanted to spend her time doing. But this wasn't for me to point out.

Over quite a few sessions, May shared that her father and her uncles were doctors, and there had been no other choice for her but to study medicine. That's all the family knew, so any other hobbies or passions in the children were not entertained. The inklings of a budding fashion designer (aha! I knew it!) were dismissed years ago and May was steered onto a career pathway that she did not choose. Her soul, which flourished in creativity, beauty and fun, had not had a chance to come out and play, and even when it naturally did, it was shut down again while the importance of doing well academically was prioritised.

After we did our work together, which involved lots of discussion around what she wanted to spend her day doing, what her values were, what activities made her light up and what limiting beliefs were standing in her way, May's mind opened to new possibilities about how she could work in a fulfilling way in all areas that interested her. Yes, May did stay in medicine, but she also made time for fashion design and started incorporating time to design clothes into her schedule. Of course, we did have to work on her schedule to ensure she had the time to do this each week; in terms of goals, we discovered that the best specialty for her in the future would be a GP. This arm of medicine gave her more flexibility around her hours, which would give her time to pursue her other loves. May was feeding her soul and not only feeling happier and healthier, but the people around her in her personal and professional life were benefitting, too – even her parents.

Often, when I watch people transform like this over time, I can't help but be reminded about areas in my life that have been lying dormant for far too long. I love to draw and handwrite – my writing is like something out of the Victorian era, with all its calligraphic strokes and overemphasised twirling letterforms. I seem to get lost in time and forget about everything else that is going on when I'm doodling in notebooks (I promise, I'm not doing this when I'm with clients). When concentrating my attention on my penmanship, I often ponder the past and why I was steered away from a creative career pathway, and whether life would be different now if I chose that life. I wonder whether I should resume art lessons again. But then, like a lot of us, life just gets in the way, and I forget about it.

When I'm talking to people I know who are unhappy or overwhelmed in their own lives, I often ask if they're doing anything that they are passionate about, that they love doing for no other reason than just because. I ask them, 'Are you feeding your soul?' This question is usually met with an odd expression, particularly from my left-brainer clients who I sense are thinking, *What on earth would that have to do with the way I am feeling? What is this woman even talking about?* It's something many of us don't think consciously about, until we become desperately stuck in negative emotions.

But, what if it is just what is missing? What if we need to get back to doing what came to us so naturally when we were younger? What if we need to do now what we did before, just for the intrinsic enjoyment of it? Just because. Many of us got caught up in what life said we should be doing, rather than what we really wanted to do. Not many of us followed what our soul was calling us to do, managing to follow our childhood dream and live our passion. For many of us, some parts of our dreams didn't quite get actualised, or maybe some parts were just forgotten.

Too many of us are artists who don't make art, readers who don't read, healers who don't heal, writers who don't write and creators who don't create. I've had clients who are footballers who don't play football, surfers who no longer surf and musicians who don't play music anymore.

Many of us are living lives that don't include a part of us that made us feel alive. We've stopped feeding our soul. As author Steven Pressfield stated, 'Most of us have two lives. The life we live, and the unlived life within us.'

Many of us have a life within us that is sitting there, waiting to be lived. And perhaps, to bring ourselves out of burnout and on to something better, we need to bring it out of hiding. Maybe it's what we need to help balance out the stressors we feel from our work, distract us from the noisy world we live in, bring us back into the present moment and light up our soul that so deeply wants us to connect with it. In fact, many people who have experienced burnout purport to getting back on track by feeding their soul with exactly what it needed – re-energising it spiritually. Many people forgot what their soul needed, and some never even knew what it needed in the first place.

To keep ourselves happy and healthy, we need to do what we're subjectively passionate about regularly. These are activities where we are in flow, when we feel in our element and when we feel most alive. The benefits we gain from these small moments of soul enrichment flow into the other areas of our lives, such as our relationships and our work. Sometimes, it's a bonus when it flows into our work, but often we can't reconcile the two. In this case, we need to find it outside of our work, as a hobby that we love. Some of my clients have fed their souls by journalling, volunteering, travelling, hiking in the forest and writing poetry. Some have fed their souls by adding a soul-enriching pillar in their business strategy, and some just feed their souls by simply sitting in a chair and listening to music. Some just give their soul the sunsets that it needs.

No one else is going to offer us a soul-enriching life; we need to create it ourselves. We can start living it now if we want to, even if it is in the smallest capacity. Dust off the guitar, get out the fishing rod, do that art class or dance the night away, even if it is just for one night. We need to resume the things we forgot we loved to do but our soul has been calling us to remember.

Considerations

What did I love to do as a child?

Is there an activity that I've always wanted to try?

Have I ever felt a 'calling' to do something?

Is there a place in the world that I've always wanted to travel?

Is there something I feel compelled to learn more about?

What are my natural gifts and talents?

Which areas of my life feel dull?

Where do I feel the need to express more of me?

What truly brings my soul alive?

What would I do if there was nothing stopping me?

How could feeding my soul more prevent burnout?

Challenge

Vision Board

Grab a range of coloured pens, magazines, scissors, glue and a large piece of cardboard. Give yourself a good chunk of time to get the creative juices flowing. Vision boards are a visual representation of yourself and are helpful in leading you to where you want to go, and it's often in the creation of them that your subconscious starts speaking to you. Usually, we overthink things way too much and often what society wants from us gets in the way of who we truly are. Vision boards typically contain a plethora of images, visuals, ideas and texts that resonate with your soul and where it wants to take you. Slowly spend the time flicking through a variety of magazines, and notice activities, colours, photos, words, quotes and people that stand out to you, that you enjoy, that inspire you or resonate with you. Cut them out and stick them to the board. Spend a few hours doing this and notice the themes that emerge. Notice if anything stands out to you and what direction your soul might be calling you to head in.

Commitment

Going forward, I commit to these new rituals to help feed my soul...

Notes

Live Your Values

'I have learned that as long as I hold fast to my beliefs and values – and follow my own moral compass – then the only expectations I need to live up to are my own.'

MICHELLE OBAMA

GABI, ONE OF my clients, had in recent years embarked on her own small business doing graphic design and social media. What started out as a fun side hustle on top of her usual day job slowly emerged into her own fully fledged business. After about a year of doing both jobs, Gabi had enough clients and income to be able to leave her unfulfilling corporate career. She now had the flexibility in her work to accommodate a new baby that was on its way. Plus, of course, her creative juices were flowing and she felt more in flow with her work. I worked with Gabi over a couple of years to help her navigate the early years of starting a family and the inevitable emotional ups and downs of running a business at the same time. Like many people us psychologists see, Gabi wasn't getting help because she was at breaking point; sometimes it's more for personal development or mental health maintenance reasons that people book in semi-regular sessions. And this is the way our therapeutic relationship worked ... until Gabi met Danielle. Then, the sessions became weekly.

Gabi met Danielle at a networking event for businesswomen, and they got on like a house on fire. A clever and business-savvy web designer who also dabbled in the social media and marketing realm, Danielle was a bucketful of knowledge and enthusiasm, and was exciting to be around. A mum herself, Danielle had been in the small business game a little longer and felt a strong professional and personal connection to Gabi – so much so that they ended up going into business together. The excitement of this new business relationship was evident when I saw Gabi in one of our sessions as she chatted through this next phase of her career.

But it didn't take too long for the excitement to wear off, and Gabi presented quite distressed in a session a few months down the track. Still in awe of this businesswoman she had connected with, and not having joined the dots yet, Gabi was not only stressed, but was questioning everything. She was feeling as though she wasn't keeping up with the work and wasn't being flexible with changes – all the very things that she prided herself on before she started her small business. Her confidence in her work had gone and she had started second-guessing herself, causing blocks in her creativity.

After a deep exploration of what had been going on during the previous few months, it was clear that there was a clashing of values with her newfound business partner.

The values that bonded them at the beginning – creativity, success and family – now were set to tear them apart. It wasn't because of anyone being wrong, it was just that the way her business partner operated out of her value system was very different to the way Gabi operated, and they were totally out of alignment. For example, many people have a strong family value. For some, this means working hard to provide for their family, and that's what Danielle did. She was up at 5am every day and in her office, sending emails and texts to her clients. She'd then take her kids to childcare, put in a huge day of work and then pick up the kids at 6pm, spend some quality time with them and then get back to work when they were in bed. Danielle thought nothing of ringing Gabi in the early hours of the morning or expecting work completed on the weekends – that's just how she rolled. She was a hard worker, efficient and successful, and she was getting a bit irked (but still in a polite way) about Gabi not keeping up with her.

Gabi had a strong family value too, but the way her family value operated was different. She would spend physical time with her kids in the morning, drop them off at school and perhaps even stay to read or help in the class. Then, she would pick up the kids at 3pm and watch them at their after-school activities. This is what she had envisioned when she thought about having a family – to have a flexible business that worked around her children so that she could spend those early years with them. She was a hard worker, efficient and successful too, but her work was secondary to spending time with her kids. The early-morning calls while she was making her kids breakfast, client meetings booked when she was watching her daughter at ballet and the expectation that work would be completed on the weekends was silently wearing Gabi down.

Instead of communicating her distress to Danielle, Gabi internalised it. Gabi felt it was her who wasn't performing well, and she decided she wasn't good enough and would be better off calling it quits. She was so exhausted that she didn't know which way to turn and had no energy to think about what the next move was. We had two people working together, values aligned, but how the values actualised in the real world were very different. No one was wrong, they were just different and misaligned, causing one person to be on the brink of burnout and ready to pull out of a successful business.

When our values are misaligned, we suffer emotionally. Values are those deeply ingrained principles we live by that inform our beliefs about the world and how we behave in it. They are like an internal compass that guides our decisions. This sounds simple enough, as we all have values that are often unconsciously navigating us through our life journey, but it becomes less simple when we realise that we've been living out of alignment with our true values for most of our life. This incongruence, along with some other factors, is likely to have contributed to our burnout. So, this raises the question ... are the values that we live by even our own?

We feel our most happy, content and alive when we are living by our own values. We've established some of our values on our own throughout our life journey, but many of us are living with the operating system of other people's values. Generally, we are predisposed to adopt the values of the people we are raised with, our family, our friends and our society in general.

Consciously knowing what our values are helps us stay on track in the present moment – in good times and when it gets tough. Knowing our values helps us feel more confident in making decisions, helps us have more of an intuitive knowing, makes us less likely to compare ourselves to others and helps us make goals for the future that fit with our unique vision. Even if we fall off track for a period because of inevitable life events, being clear on our values makes it much easier to reconnect with them.

So, how can we define our own values? We need to firstly think back to the most meaningful moments in our life. These are moments where we would have been feeling a positive emotion but also feeling fulfilled and at ease. These moments would have been meaningful for a reason, so reflecting on what we were doing and why these moments meant so much is important.

When thinking about what our values could naturally be, it's useful to pay attention to the people around us. Not only the people close to us, but the people outside of our immediate circle, such as colleagues, leaders in the areas of our interests, celebrities or our favourite artists. Take note of the qualities of people we admire, respect, pay attention to or who inspire us. Think about why they resonate with us so much, and what internal qualities they have that we may like to embody.

It also pays to think about who and what annoys us (this is usually quite an easy task – for me anyway). What is it about certain people in our life (including those outside of our immediate circle) that gets our goat? What are they mirroring back to us? Is a person irritating us because of what they do and how they are contradict our values, or are they strongly embodying values that we share but that we have yet to actualise within ourselves? Chances are that most of us get irked by certain successful celebrities, and it's valuable to ask ourselves: why?

We also need to remember that our values can change over time and are influenced throughout our life journey by different experiences. People change, and so do their values.

The most important thing to remember is that whenever our values are compromised by others, or even by ourselves, or when we're heading off on another person's pathway that isn't really our own, our brain and body will be responding in some way. It won't feel right. We'll likely feel uneasy and discontent, and sometimes we might not be able to pinpoint why we feel like that.

Checking in regularly on our values is a must. We need to make sure that our daily behaviours and actions are congruent with our values. Next time your brain and body are whispering to you that something has gone awry, refer to your values and ask, 'Is what I'm doing truly aligned with my values?' If not, steer yourself in the other direction and make different choices.

Considerations

What are my personal values?

What are my family values?

What are my work values?

What are my cultural values?

Are these values truly my own? Or have they been instilled in me by others? Those values that don't resonate with me need to go, so what values am I left with?

What do I need to add or remove from my life to reflect these values?

How could living in alignment with my values prevent burnout?

Challenge

Values-Based Living

Think of the four or five values that are your top core values – the ones that you know are deal-breakers for you in life. Write them somewhere you'll see them every day, such as your phone's lock screen, on a Post-it Note on your computer, with a marker on your fridge or with lipstick on your mirror. Look at these values every morning and let their meaning sink in. Operationalise what they mean to you and think through the actions you need to take throughout the day to align with these values. Think of the behaviours you can engage in to tick off these values. In tricky moments where you are struggling to make the right decision, look at these values and see if your answer comes to you. Notice how you feel as a result of these values living through you consciously.

Commitment

Going forward, I commit to these new rituals to encourage values-based living...

Notes

Create Healthy Habits

'When it comes to health and wellbeing, regular exercise is about as close to a magic potion as you can get.'

THICH NHAT HANH

APART FROM JUMPING into water any chance I get, being physically active in some shape or form is a necessity for me. Not just for my physical health, but my sanity. I'm no gym junkie and I have plenty of wobbly bits, but my morning and evening exercise sessions are non-negotiable – no matter how busy I am during the day. It's only lightning that will stop me and, even then, just for a moment. When I feel that my (and my dog's) life is no longer at risk from being struck by a lightning bolt, and I'm comfortable that it's gone, I will head straight back outside again. Not much can stop us and our walkies.

Anyone who was once a physically active person but isn't anymore (intentionally or not) will confidently attest to the negative impact this has had on them, physically and psychologically. Many of us forget that there are so many actions and behaviours that can change the way we feel. This is true not only in the moment when we're feeling a negative emotion (remember, it's not the stress that matters, it's what we do with it), but in a preventative capacity – to keep us physically and psychologically healthy. If we have a foundation of good health, we have more resilience to deal with life when the going gets tough.

There is a plethora of research on how good exercise is for our physical health. It protects against many chronic diseases, lowers blood pressure, improves heart health, maintains muscle strength, improves joint pain and increases life span. But there's also a wealth of studies that have shown the positive impact exercise has on our brain.[13] This is why, no matter what psychological health issue my clients present with, I always make sure that before they head out my door, I have enquired about their physical activity levels and recommended exercise to boost their wellbeing. I bet there is not a psychologist around the place who would think otherwise.

Exercise is the single *best* thing we can do to balance out our negative emotions and reset ourselves. Physical activity improves our mood – while we're exercising and also afterwards. Not only does it improve negative mood states such as anxiety and depressive-type symptoms, but it also increases positive mood states such as revitalisation, and feelings of wellbeing such as happiness. Exercise releases endorphins into our body, hence why we feel so euphoric, happy and energised after exercising.

Being physically active on an ongoing basis can also help raise our self-worth, self-esteem and confidence. This is particularly apt in moments of our life where an incident has happened that has dented our self-worth (e.g. when we feel burned out). It doesn't take much to rock our self-esteem, and if we have other behaviours that we engage in that can boost it this keeps everything balanced. I've had clients who've been in the midst of immense challenges – from the emotional turmoil of dealing with a partner who has had an affair to legal battles over businesses to workplace conflicts that have completely shaken their confidence and ripped out their self-worth – who say that keeping up their exercise routine was the thing that kept them going.

One of the common benefits of exercise is stress relief, as well as stress resilience. Not only does it reduce physical stress that builds up during the day, but also mental stress. The 'runner's high' we feel after moving our bodies is associated with a drop in stress hormones. Because it helps alleviate stress, exercise makes us feel more resilient the following day to cope with new stressors. Another bonus of exercising is better sleep. Good sleep allows our body to rest and replenish itself for the next day. During this time, our long-term memory can consolidate everything from the day, which will also improve learning. Physical activity has been shown to help with sleep.

Creating healthy habits moves beyond exercise to

any sort of behaviour or action we can take to help shift an emotion to the positive. Earlier on I discussed the importance of emotions and how important it is to feel them. Then, when we have given ourselves a chance to feel and process them, we have the opportunity to do something to shift the way we feel.

Research shows that more active activities such as exercise can be effective for recovery from mental health issues, whether that be anxiety or depression. Among the myriad healthy recovery activities we could do, it's the active ones (physical activities, social activities and creative activities) that are more helpful for improving wellbeing than more passive activities (such as watching TV). It might be a hobby that challenges us and requires effort or mastery, such as learning to play a musical instrument or learning a new language. These types of activities keep us in a 'flow state', which means that we're more engaged in the present moment, challenged by the activity and distracted from the stressors in our world. These types of activities help to replenish our depleted resources.

Us human beings are pack animals, so it's no wonder that enjoyable social activities are high on the list in keeping us psychologically healthy. Studies have shown time and time again that social activities are an important component of stress reduction for people.[14] Whether it's chatting to friends, joining a club or talking online, the regular chance to connect, debrief and get the support we need for what we are going through is crucial.

There are other things that affect our mood, such as the food and beverages we consume. If we were to be honest with ourselves, would we say our food intake is impacting us in a negative way and contributing to us feeling more negative emotions, or is our intake making us feel better?

It's always helpful to think about the little healthy things that we can proactively incorporate into our lives because our brain can be reactive in the moment. If we don't have some healthy options lined up then, guess what? Our brain will take us to some unhealthy things to help soothe us. If you've ever had a switch in your brain that turns off after drinking two glasses of wine after a tough day and makes you drink the whole bottle, you will understand what I'm saying here. Put the healthy things in place so that they are there all the time and part of the healthy foundation in which you usually operate. If you slip up now and again, don't judge yourself – just get back to the healthy things the next day. It doesn't take much for stress to build up in our lives, so it's important that we have actions and behaviours that we incorporate into our day to balance these out.

Considerations

If I were to be honest with myself, am I living a healthy life?

Am I using some unhealthy coping mechanisms for negative emotions that may be making things worse for me?

If I was to get help, what would this look like?

Am I physically active enough? If not, what could I start doing to improve this?

Does my nutritional intake need some work? If so, what could I start doing to improve this?

Am I spending enough time in nature?

Am I socialising enough?

Am I doing any creative activities that give my mind a break from my stressors?

Is there anything I used to do that made me feel healthy and energetic that I can incorporate back into my life?

How could doing more healthy things in my life prevent burnout?

Challenge

Exercise Ritual

No matter how physically active you are, pick one exercise activity that is the most enjoyable to you (one that you don't currently do). It could be doing some stretching on your garden lawn, getting your bicycle out for a ride around your suburb, walking the dog at sunset, pushing the kids on their scooters around the park or even joining a neighbourhood dance class, but be specific about what it is. Now, look in your diary and find three 30-minute slots of time, either in the morning before you start your day or at the end of it. Then, book those exercise sessions into those time slots as though they are as important as a meeting or an appointment. Tell the people around you that you are doing this so they can hold you accountable. For one month, do this activity. Note any physical or psychological changes you notice during and after this time period.

Commitment

Going forward,
I commit to these
new rituals to
help support
my physical and
psychological
health...

Notes

Sleep Well

'Sleep is an investment in the energy you need to be effective tomorrow.'

TOM RATH

IF I RECEIVED a dollar for every time a client mentioned they were having trouble sleeping, I would be a very rich woman. (Come to think of it, I do get a dollar for every time a client mentions they are having trouble sleeping, as this is my job.) But I don't resonate with the rich bit. I think most psychologists would agree with me that sleep is troublesome for many of their clients, particularly those who've been under chronic stress for a long period of time (they'd agree about the not being rich bit, too).

You'd think that if you were burned out you'd have no trouble sleeping – that you're so tired and exhausted that sleep is the only thing on your mind. But this is not always the case. Many people who have experienced burnout have had problematic sleep for a long period of time leading up to it, and then the burnout period has elicited a host of unhelpful sleeping habits (e.g. napping) and routines. At the time these habits and routines might be helpful for burnout recovery but going forward, not so much. We want to prevent getting into a sleep-debt situation again, so it's imperative that a good sleep is on the top of our list to perform our best in life.

We all know what not enough sleep feels like. You know, those nights where we stayed out too late, binge-watched too many episodes of our favourite TV series or stayed up all night to watch the tennis. We know how abysmal the next day feels and how much less of a person we feel (and how much more concealer we have to use, or maybe that's just me). We're tired, grumpy, can't think straight and even have trouble stringing sentences together. The fatigue affects everything. The only thing we're destined to do after feeling like this is go straight to bed without speaking to anyone. That's the safest thing to do – for everyone. But we reflect on these all-nighters as one-offs. They don't do much harm, and a nice early sleep the following night can usually fill the bucket and help us get back to functioning like a human once more.

But pulling all-nighters once or twice a year isn't what causes the tiredness, exhaustion and sleeping problems that are so common for many of us. It's the sleep deprivation and interrupted sleep that creep into our nights on a regular basis, accumulating over time to create a sleep debt that is so prevalent in our modern society.

Sleeping is more than just shutting our eyes and opening them again seven hours later. Sleeping is a time for the mind and body to relax, recharge, reset and rejuvenate. We may feel like we've been in a deep comatose state where there hasn't been much happening, but there's a whole lot of brain partying going on when we're sleeping and a clean-up to boot. If we're not getting the sleep we need, we are depriving ourselves of vital processes that are necessary to revitalise us for the next day. It's safe to say that we do not fare well without quality sleep. Yet too many of us are not getting enough of it.

We're wired to sleep when it's dark and be awake when it's light (shocking, I know). This would have made total sense to our ancestors who didn't want to be out and about late, at risk of being taken down by a predator. Us humans fare better when we are tucked away to rest at night. Sleeping helps us to conserve energy and consolidate memory. There are four distinct stages of sleep: N1, N2 and N3 of non-rapid eye movement (NREM) sleep, followed by rapid eye movement (REM) sleep. The processes involved in these stages make sure that our body is well rested, and that everything is put where it needs to be in the brain so that it can perform at its best the next day.

If we're sleeping well, this lessens stress's impact and improves our cognitive function and our performance in general. We're always more refreshed after a good night's sleep (and, to be honest, often a lot nicer to be around).

Like many of our bodily functions, sleep is governed by a circadian rhythm. This natural sleep cycle gives us an urge to wake at a particular time each day and, along with a build-up of accumulated sleep pressure, fall asleep at a particular time. But since the invention of the light bulb, smart devices and modern stressors, we tend to ignore all of this and do what we feel like in the evenings for our own entertainment – much to the detriment of our sleep and our mental health.

It's important that we make sure our sleep is as on point as it can possibly be. Yes, there are always going to be disruptions to our sleep; there will be moments where we wake in the night worrying about the presentation tomorrow, the bills we must pay or an uncomfortable conversation with our partner, or to check the kiddies haven't been taken by a sabre-toothed tiger (oops, that was our ancestors). It's normal for us to wake throughout the night, and in most cases (even sometimes without our awareness) we will drift back to sleep reasonably quickly.

To maximise our quality of sleep, there are some healthy sleeping habits we can incorporate into our life. In terms of our sleep environment, our brain needs a safe, relaxing and familiar environment to let its guard down and turn sleep on for us. The Danish have a term called *hygge*, which means a cosy environment that is created to elicit relaxation. In the context of sleep, this involves warm blankets, clean bedsheets, a comfy bed and soft pillows, all of which we can happily snuggle into come bedtime. The environment in which we sleep needs to be at a reasonable temperature – the Goldilocks room temperature for us humans is about 18 degrees Celsius. Our brain also prefers no noise, and the room needs to be dark. Those pesky little standby lights on TVs and the gazillion flickering notifications going off on our phone can be disturbing. Even though we might be asleep on some level, our brain is still often tuning into what's going on in our room, house and even outside. So, give it the calming space that it needs.

On a personal front, we'll find that some of our habits might need a bit of tweaking to improve our sleep. No judgement if we're partaking in any of these behaviours, but it's worth trying to eliminate them if we're trying to count sheep way too often. It always astonishes me when I'm working with a client who has chronic sleeping problems and they tell me they have an espresso or energy drink before bed (I'm not joking, this has happened numerous times). Caffeine before bed is usually not conducive to a good sleep, so try to stick to caffeinated drinks before lunchtime. Caffeine has a half-life of approximately six hours, so 50 per cent of it is still left in our system six hours after we drink it. The same goes for what we eat. Try to have heavier meals a few hours before bedtime, be careful of the sugar hit from alcoholic drinks and steer clear of the red cordial. Bouncing off the walls before we go to bed is not what we want to be doing when we have an alarm set for 6am.

Our sleep routine in the lead-up to bed is very important, too, and it's a bonus benefit if the routine is roughly the same each night (I know, BORING, but I said *roughly*). If we have a nice sleep routine with some soothing rituals in the lead-up to going to bed, we are signalling to our brain that it's nearly time for sleep and it needs to get prepared for it. It's best that we go to bed at roughly the same time each night, particularly when we get up at the same time. Start the wind-down an hour before bedtime. This may involve finishing up watching TV, turning off our devices, taking a warm shower or bath, turning off the lights (or at least turning them down very low), going to the toilet, cleaning our teeth and then lying in bed reading a book with a softly lit lamp on the bedside table. In other words, it does not mean writing emails chaotically until 10pm, lying in bed watching movies, turning off the light and then checking Instagram, TikTok and Facebook. It does not mean this at all.

Having healthy sleep is crucial to our functioning and will help us cope with any negative emotions we may feel in the future. As adults, we need to create a personal routine that is conducive to sleep by giving our brain what it needs to turn on sleep.

Considerations

Do I feel energised and restored in the morning?

Do feel I tired during the day on a regular basis?

Do I have to drink more than three coffees a day to keep me alert?

Do I have trouble going to sleep at night?

Do I have to drink alcohol or take medications to get me to sleep?

Do I wake up frequently during the night?

Do I get close to the recommended hours of sleep a night?

Is my environment conducive to a good night's sleep?

Do I have a wind-down ritual before bedtime?

Do I go to bed and wake up at roughly the same time every day?

Do I need to improve my sleep habits?

How could sleeping better prevent burnout?

Challenge

Sleep Reset

Start with choosing one specific time in the morning that you know you usually have to get up at (e.g. 7am), and set your alarm for this time on an ongoing basis (even on the weekend). Then, on the first evening, only go to bed when your eyes are tired. Keep yourself busy (even if its super late) and only get into your bed when you know you will fall asleep. If you stay awake for longer than five minutes, turn on a side lamp and read until your eyes are tired. Then, only turn off the light when you are about to fall asleep again. Don't look at your phone, a clock or any other backlit device in this time. Just read quietly until your eyes are tired again. Get up at your alarm time, unless you wake earlier. Repeat the same process every night to reset your sleep rhythm. Over time, you will find that you will start going to bed earlier and earlier. Notice how this feels after a month and check in to see whether you are feeling more refreshed.

Commitment

Going forward, I commit to these new rituals to improve the quality of my sleep...

Notes

Talk Out Loud

'The single biggest problem in communication is the illusion that it has taken place.'

GEORGE BERNARD SHAW

A PREVIOUS CLIENT of mine, Glenda, was deputy principal of a high school and had been enjoying her role for many years. She was deeply committed to her job, the staff and the students. Her face lit up when she talked about her work, as well as the school community she had the privilege of being part of for nearly a decade. Like many school leaders and teachers, she worked long hours. She always arrived early and left late, was always 'on' during the school's open hours, covered lessons because of staffing issues and worked well into the night to catch up on her own work that she couldn't do in her increasingly 'troubleshooting' role as a deputy during the day.

Glenda's day was already full of dealing with people and navigating the complexities of staff and student issues, but she never described it in a negative way. She spoke of fulfilling-but-full days where, by the time she arrived home from work, kicked off her shoes and flopped on the couch, her tiredness was from the sheer exhaustion of being 'on' all day without a break, rather than anything else.

By the time I had the pleasure of working with Glenda, she was still feeling like this and described her working environment and personal home life in a positive way. Being such a bubbly and shiny woman, she never described anything in a negative way. But she had noticed that she was becoming more exhausted and a little anxious. Her workload was increasing and her leadership role, albeit gratifying, was taking her away from the teaching roles that she loved dearly. All of this had been simmering away for a little while. It was 'nothing major', as Glenda reported, but enough that she was taking notice.

We worked together slowly over a few sessions with her feeling calmer, more confident and more in control to steer herself in the right direction going forward. I didn't see Glenda for about two years after that, until a whirlwind of a new principal arrived on the school scene and, with a wave of a magic (narcissist's) wand, destroyed all the hard work Glenda had done, along with her calmness, her confidence and, of course, her control. Glenda had never experienced anything like it, nor had she ever been on the end of the wrath of someone with such destructive personality traits.

A whole host of new problems emerged that impacted Glenda psychologically. An unreasonable workload to manage that was ignored and dismissed in meetings, along with being micromanaged, lied to, controlled and gaslighted for months, on top of her usual duties (which we'd worked damn hard on to balance, mind you), led to Glenda becoming a very burned-out woman. Sessions with Glenda soon became entirely about how to deal with a problematic personality in the workplace, and why communication is key.

We need to be able to communicate freely with people in our lives. Obviously, it's great to communicate about normal day-to-day happenings as well as positive things that are going on, but we also need to discuss issues that are on our minds and causing us negative emotions. We don't want emotions and unsaid conversations bottled up, nor any yelling when we reach breaking point.

Once we've worked out that we're feeling a certain way about something in our life, and pinpointed something that needs to be changed in order for us to feel better, it's crucial that we communicate this to the people who need to know. There's no point in having a conversation in your head in the shower or while you're driving in your car. These internal-dialogue conversations are often when we seem to be our most articulate (with sarcastic wit to boot), but they sadly don't seem to come out like this in real life. These conversations need to be had as quickly as possible with whoever needs to hear them so that we can solve any problems. It's even more important that we communicate how we're feeling to the people who may have played a part in the situation that has caused us to feel negative emotions.

Some of these conversations will be very uncomfortable indeed, but without them, problems linger and stay unresolved, causing unnecessary distress. That's what can lead to burnout: a build-up of emotions that haven't been shifted as the communication hasn't been had.

Communication, at its simplest, is about transmitting information. It's sending and receiving messages with the people in our lives. We hope that our messages to others are received and absorbed, and vice versa. But it's an imperfect world and for a variety of reasons, this doesn't always happen. Sometimes people don't understand what we are saying and sometimes they can become defensive. In many cases we decide not to say anything at all, yet we believe that the person should know what we want to say. Unless we are talented enough to transmute our message to the people around us through some sort of psychokinesis, we need to say what we think out loud to prevent burnout in the future. We need to be in an ebb and flow with the world around us, which includes the people in it. Communication is so important.

Boundaries also deserve a special mention here. In fact, they deserve their own special book due to the high importance we should place on them. After all the hard work we might have done to recover and heal from burnout – all the psychological hard yards that we've put in to come back better than ever – if we don't protect this, then guess what? Everything will creep back in. And that's where boundaries come in, or need to be put up.

Like a fence around the property we live in keeps us and the things that are of value to us safe, boundaries keep us protected. They keep us in alignment with what we know is extremely important to us, what makes us feel good, what we want to stay with us and what we know we need in our life to be happy. Without the fence, or the boundaries, the external world, and all that comes with that, can possibly wreak havoc.

The thing about boundaries is that they are our own responsibility to communicate. We need to think hard about what we want and don't want in our life. If we don't know these things and can't communicate them to others, people will continue to do what they want – even when it doesn't work for us. It's only us who can say 'yes', or 'no'. And as simple as those one-syllable words sound, 'no' in particular is the most difficult, especially if we're partial to saying 'yes' way too much.

Setting boundaries with other people can come in many forms, but a simple formula is stating how you feel, why you feel like that and what you need to have happen. For example, 'I'm feeling really overwhelmed at the moment because my workload is too much given the timeframe, and I would like to have a conversation about how to ease the pressure.' Another example that might be useful on the home front: 'I'm feeling really frustrated; I've got so much to do around the house and all the jobs are building up, so can we talk about other people around the house taking on some of the household chores?' Or even a social example: 'I'm feeling so exhausted lately because I have a heavy workload and I'm working far too late every night, so I can't go out with you all tonight as I need to have a night in to rest and recharge.'

Of course, an even simpler boundary statement is saying 'NO' with a big full stop at the end of it. We can say that as a complete sentence, sans any sort of explanation, and that's our prerogative. Many of us on our journey of establishing firm boundaries in our life still feel a little uncomfortable with not giving that extra information to explain why we need the change to happen. But if you're comfortable with just 'no', then good for you!

The more we set boundaries, the more we can do it in a calm, firm, confident and respectful way, and the better we will feel. We will become more aligned with what we truly want in life and start feeling better ... but not immediately. It's tricky before it becomes easy, and we need to prepare ourselves for this. Sometimes, we're looking forward to a massive emotional release or an abundance of freedom and a chance to be just ourselves again, but we find that we end up sitting in an emotional soup of guilt and regret for saying anything at all. The people we placed boundaries with might be shocked, disappointed, rejected, hurt or sad, and it may feel like it's our fault. The guilt is so heavy that we're tempted to backtrack so everyone can just be at peace again. But if we do that, we'll be the one who isn't at peace and is back on the overwhelmed train to burnout again.

So, what do we do when we've finally built up the courage to say a few words that mean 'I'm important', 'I count', 'I matter' and 'this is what I need to be my best self' *and* keep our boundaries firmly in place? We stop feeling responsible for other people's feelings. It's up to other people to be self-aware of their own feelings, process them and regulate them (just like I've been teaching you). You will often find that those who kick up a fuss about your boundaries are those you need to protect yourself from most fiercely. If they are having trouble with your boundaries, they need to get their own help with that (tell them to come and see me). But seriously, we can't make other people feel anything; that's on them to process and make sense of. For the most part, people are respectful of our boundaries and will learn eventually what our needs are.

My client Glenda had to do this very thing. She toyed with the idea of quitting the job that she once loved, but over time grew to be more assertive and articulate in the way she communicated with her principal. Through calling meetings between the two of them and clearly stating boundaries that communicated how she felt and why, and also holding ground on behaviours she saw as unacceptable, she was able to communicate to the principal about what she wouldn't put up with. It wasn't always easy – and the principal did still dismiss her at times – but from a therapeutic point of view, these conversations were being had, which was better for Glenda. It is still a work in progress – as all of our stories are.

Talking out loud also includes communicating our stories. It means talking to those around us and sharing how we feel, what our thoughts are and what we're going through. This not only helps us connect with others, but it allows others to connect with us. We're wired to be connected to others, so for us to navigate the trials and tribulations of life in a healthy way, we need a village to talk to – this includes family, friends, colleagues, wise elders, mentors and professionals. Good communication can facilitate the support we need to heal and prevent burnout.[14] Ask yourself: is there something I need to say out loud?

Considerations

Do I need to talk out loud to people more often? At home? At work?

Would seeing a mental health professional, a coach or a mentor be useful to me?

Who are the people closest to me who I can debrief with, get support from or talk honestly with?

Do I need to be more vulnerable with those around me?

Are there particular boundaries that I need to put up that would be helpful to me? Who would they be with?

What would be beneficial to me if I communicated these boundaries?

What will happen if I don't?

Do I have any unsaid conversations happening in my mind? Who are they directed at?

If there was nothing to stop me, what would I say to other people?

How could communicating more with the people around me prevent burnout?

Challenges

Boundary Setting

Think of a person in your life who you are constantly saying 'yes' to, when deep down you really want to say 'no'. A good idea here is to reflect on your values, and notice if they may be compromised anywhere. Sit in the negative feelings of any boundaries being crossed, and think about what needs to happen to make these feelings disappear. Arrange a meeting with this person in your life and, during the conversation, calmly let them know how you are feeling (using an 'I' statement), let them know why (focusing on the behaviour) and then let them know what needs to happen next (in terms of actions). For example, 'I am feeling overwhelmed because I have work projects on at the moment, so I won't be able to take on that task right now'. Notice how it feels to get this off your chest.

Commitment

Going forward,
I commit to
these new rituals
to implement
stronger
boundaries
in my life...

Notes

Stuff Around

‘We don’t stop playing because we grow old; we grow old because we stop playing.’

GEORGE BERNARD SHAW

MY HUSKY CROSS, Chilly, knows that upstairs in our house is the perfect place for a zoomie. While usually relegated to the first storey with its shiny wooden (and slippery for fluffy toes) floorboards, she, with defiance, never misses a chance to bolt upstairs when no one is watching. When the ceiling above us is rumbling and thudding like a thunderstorm, and Chilly is not lying in her bed, we know that a golden zoomie opportunity has been found.

For those of you who are not familiar with a zoomie, it's a frenetic, unexplainable burst of energy that is spontaneous and done for no reason other than pure enjoyment. For Chilly, it involves sprinting around various rooms of the house with mad delight and jumping on all the furniture, knocking every pillow and rug into the air as she speeds around. This could last a good five minutes or so. Given she's a 30-kilogram dog, it's always best for us to keep out of the pathway of a Chilly zoomie, particularly if we're wanting to keep our leg bones intact. It is nothing but pure delight watching these bursts of energy and I can never help but laugh.

Spontaneous play is something us adult humans are hopeless at, quite frankly. And if there is an adult who is quite good at being silly (or doing a zoomie), we quickly call them a clown or an idiot. But given it's the perfect antidote to stress, perhaps incorporating some more fun or play into our adult lives is something we all need to be thinking about. This is particularly so in the world we live in, where it feels like we are in a never-ending 'permacrisis' (permanent crisis) that keeps on eliciting more negative emotions within us. Being prepared with a bag of play tricks to balance us out with some positive emotions is just what the doctor, or our friendly psychologist, is ordering for us.

The thing about young kids (and my dog) is that most of them know how to have a good time. They are spontaneous, imaginative and don't care who is watching. They think about what they want to do for fun, and then they simply do it. They can lose themselves in enjoyable activities for a long time and even in the seemingly silliest moments have a diminished consciousness of self. It's only as we start getting feedback from the outside world that we start veering away from what we are inherently attracted to, in terms of play and fun, and conforming to society. We start quite early aligning ourselves to what the people around us – our parents, siblings, friends, people at school and society in general – deem appropriate. As a result, the activities we naturally felt drawn towards for fun slowly slip away. Then, we become adults (aka the fun police).

Acting like a child now and again and engaging in play is something that us adults should do more of. So much so that many organisations are engaging people to teach adult play to their teams, as well as incorporating a sense of play into office design. Play has been shown to increase teamwork, innovation and connection, boost creativity and productivity, help problem-solving and prevent burn-out.[15,16] It gives us back a spark, especially when it feels like parts of life are trying to take our light away from us.

Play has been shown to change our mood. Obviously, in the moment we're often smiling or laughing, which has a bundle of benefits. It increases happiness, momentarily as well as over time, when we build more of it into our busy schedules. It also reduces stress and anxiety. It's hard to engage in worrisome thoughts when we're in the middle of a game of charades, cackling at a funny meme or listening to a friend share the story of an unfortunate drunk moment. Play has also been shown to improve relationships, as it aids in connecting with the people in our lives. When we're playing, we're totally in the moment and engaged with that person – even if the person happens to be ourselves. The benefits of stuffing around to assist in the boosting of mood and alleviation of negative emotions needs to be seriously considered. It acts as a balancing out of sorts.

For most of us grown-ups, play is seriously missing in our life. I often ask people where they can purposefully prioritise play in their lives. The sad thing is, many draw a blank on where to start. When prompted to think about what they once did for fun, way back when, they might come up with a couple of things, but it was so long ago that they feel like a bit of a wally for starting up that activity again.

The term 'play' is hard to define because there's no one-size-fits-all form of play. In an adult world that revolves around outcomes, achieving and competing, play is anything but. It's about pleasure and doing something that has no other purpose than just that. It's usually voluntary (so it's totally up to us what we want to do) and it's subjective (what one person finds fun is another person's God-awful horror). Some people hate cats, but I could crack myself up all by myself watching funny cat video compilations for fun. Others would prefer a more toned-down chuckle with their friends that might bore the life out of some people. Other people have a favourite comedian they listen to that others simply don't get.

Knowing what feels fun, what makes us laugh and what makes us lose ourselves a little is important. It could be moving our body as a form of play, playing with things as a type of play or using our imagination for play. It could be celebratory play or storytelling play. It could just be rolling around on the floor in a rough-and-tumble type of play. It's our play and we can do with it what we want to.

If we're having trouble thinking about what on earth we could be playful with, we can think back to our childhood and reconnect with those past joys. Yes, we can still play LEGO and yes, we can still watch old movies. What were our natural talents that we were drawn to when we were younger? What got us so excited as a child? There are fun and play opportunities everywhere, but we must go looking. Pets, kids, movies, music, memes, playgrounds, adventure parks, balls, feathers, toys, jokes, stories, reels, farts and funny people. Look for the funny people! Even in the most difficult moments in life, we can still find humour and something playful in it.

Let's start giving ourselves permission to be more playful. Watch the energy shift within ourselves and the people around us when we start getting a bit more playful. Strip off the fear and sense of self and incorporate more play, mucking around and fun into your life. It's the antidote to stress that's more than a little childish.

Considerations

Do I laugh often?

Do I feel playful with other people in my life?

Do I crack jokes or show my silly side to others?

Do I have a good sense of humour? If so, do I show it?

Did I use to be fun when I was younger?

Do I feel more productive when I've stopped to have some fun?

Have I noticed that I'm more creative when I've had a laugh or done something silly?

Do I look for things to find humour in?

Have I ever gained any insight or had a light-bulb moment when I am doing fun activities?

Do I feel relaxed and re-energised after a social event with mates?

Have I felt less stressed after a fun day out with friends?

How could incorporating more play in my life prevent burnout?

Challenge

Comedy

There's nothing like a comedy show to distract you and energise you at the same time. Check out any local comedy shows in your area and organise a night out with your workmates or friends. Just go there and have a good time with each other. The next day, reflect on what happened while you were at the show, paying particular attention to what your mind did, what your stress levels were, where your thoughts took you, your energy levels and the connection of the group you were with. Notice the positive benefits just a few hours of playfulness, humour and fun had on you and the people around you.

Commitment

Going forward,
I commit to these
new rituals to
invite more play
into my life...

Notes

Be Thankful

'"Enough" is a feast.'

BUDDHIST PROVERB

I'VE PICKED UP my children after school pretty much every day for the past 12 years. One massive bonus of having my own business is that I've been able to shape my work around the school drop-off and pick-up schedules for all these years. Of course, this ability to have a personal taxi driver every day has likely been taken for granted by my kids. I'm sure they are unconsciously grateful, because they are positively horrified when, on occasion, I do get stuck and they have to take the lengthy bus trip home. For those who know teenagers, they tend to be absolutely dying of starvation by 3pm, usually have somewhere to be ten minutes after they get home and have mostly held on for dear life for the toilet all day. So it's terribly inconvenient for them not to be driven home (insert eye roll).

I've always found the car ride useful for conversations with my kids. It gives me, as a parent, the time to have a little chat with them and get a recap of their day before they stumble in the front door and disappear. In the car, you have them all to yourself, which is very useful for talking to teenagers who don't want a face-to-face conversation with their parents anymore – they can safely have a sideways chat in the car and give you the side eye without you even noticing.

Now that my kids are older, one of my teens still gives me a detailed recap of her day, from the minute she arrived at school to the moment I picked her up (which, to be honest, takes most of the car ride home), whereas my other teen, who finds school to be anything but worthwhile, can summarise his whole day with, 'it was decent'. On many occasions, when I'm squeezing for a little more information about how the day went and I'm getting the feeling he doesn't want to do a full recap, I simply ask, 'What was the best part of your day?' or 'What are you grateful for?' Without fail, he replies, 'eating food'. And we both give each other the side eye in the car, with a smile. It's a small win, a small appreciation, a small acknowledgement that there are some good things that happen in a day that scored zero on a teenage boy's Richter scale. And with that comes a small shift in the way he feels.

To be honest, I'm sure he's not the only one with 'eating food' as the highlight of their day. But it's easy for all of us to get caught up in the negative emotions that a difficult day might elicit. As I mentioned previously, all those negative emotions we feel throughout our day are valid, but if we don't do anything with them, they can stagnate us and change the way we view the world. They accumulate and we don't only almost become the emotion, but we see the world through the lens of what we've almost become (grumpy old man, anyone?). Then that's all we see, and all that we inevitably feel we get back from the world.

On top of our not-so-helpful 'modern human' ability to build up our emotions and store them like a squirrel storing nuts for the winter, we also carry our ancestors' (more helpful) negativity bias. This useful survival tool enabled us to be in a constant state of scanning our environments so any potential negative threat (e.g. sabre-toothed tiger) didn't kill us. But if we are constantly looking for threats, thinking about the threats and predicting the threats of the future, and feeling the emotions associated with this impending doom, then guess what? We're not going to be in a good mood.

So, in many cases, the feelings state many of us are in is that happiness is somewhere in the future. Sometimes we think we know what will make us happy: not having to work, no more worries, perhaps a partner, lots of money and, of course, a Maserati. Everyone looks happy in a Maserati, right? Many of us believe that if we get these things in the future, we will be happy as a result.

One of the things that us humans have in common is that we all want to be happy. But we see it way into the future, and we make it conditional on something happening to us or for us. We deny the power we have over our feelings in the now. Our never-ending pursuit of future-based happiness is just that: a pursuit. It's always a little out of reach. Today's emotions get in the way and it feels like we're never quite there. And even when we do reach happiness, it's fleeting and we move the goal posts further into the future again. Even the people with a Maserati do this (believe me). There are plenty of people who do manage to get what they think they want, yet are still not happy. There are also people who go through a tremendous amount of adversity and are very happy. What this shows is that happiness doesn't relate to everything working out or us getting what we think will make us happy. Happiness is, in fact, created by having gratitude for what is happening in our life right now. Even when it's tough or when we're feeling a mix of negative emotions.

Gratitude is an emotion that involves expressing appreciation for what we have in the present moment. It's thankfulness for what is. Yes, we can be grateful for the weather, the food we eat, the red shoes that are stocked in our size (a very valid appreciation in my opinion) and the people we have in our lives, but I'm talking about gratitude on a deeper level, with an ongoing habit of feeling the enormity of it.

When I'm working with my clients, I often suggest

a gratitude ritual as homework – not only as part of the healing process, but as something that they can do on an ongoing basis to slowly rewire their brain to get more of a balanced perspective of their life. I'm usually met with an eye roll or an 'are you serious?' face because the simplicity of it seems almost insulting. It seems up there with the 'think positive' advice that others give us when we feel anything but. But I urge everyone to explore the power of gratitude from this day forward.

More research is gathering on the power of gratitude. It's been shown to not only boost happiness over time but is strongly related to all aspects of wellbeing. It improves energy levels, optimism, self-esteem and connection. It's also been shown to decreases stress, anxiety and depression. Gratitude is associated with a lower risk of nicotine, alcohol and drug dependence as well as improved self-care, including a greater likelihood of exercising.[17,18,19] All these things are usually on my hit list when it comes to psychological advice.

When we don't stop and literally count our blessings, our negativity bias will lure our thoughts to the dark side as a way to keep us safe, wary and, quite frankly, in a state of doom and gloom. Then, unfortunately, in a 'woo woo' sort of way, we tend to manifest more of that. Engaging in gratitude on purpose, which helps our brain to refocus on the good stuff in the present, affects how we perceive reality, so not being grateful can block us. Without consciously ritualising gratitude, we may not get the balanced feelings we need to prevent burnout.

On a chirpy note, gratitude may be one of the most overlooked tools that we all have access to every day, and we can start using it straight away. It doesn't take much time, it's cheap, we don't need anyone to help us do it and we don't even need to read a book about it. Like the famous Nike slogan suggests, we've got to 'just do it'.

We can be grateful, appreciative, thankful, stoked or even just incredibly stunned by the awesomeness of a very specific thing that is happening right now. Allow the release of emotions while you are thinking about what you're grateful for; feel them. Yes, we can appreciate our kids or be grateful for our home, but we need to purposefully try to be intentional with our observations of our environment. I want more adjectives, more descriptions and more details of the intricate moments of the day. We need to notice the dulcet tones of the artist of our favourite song as it plays in our headphones on the train on the way home from work. We need to appreciate the cheeky and handsome barista with the smooth Italian accent who made our large soy milk cappuccino. We need to feel thankful for our best friend direct messaging us the perfect fainting goats video on Instagram at the exact time we needed to be cheered up.

We need to proclaim the winning micro moments of our everyday life and reflect on them in our gratitude ritual – even if the rest of the day needed to go in the bin. And if we get stuck finding what to be grateful for now and then, there's always 'eating food'.

Considerations

Do I tend to focus on the negatives most of the time?

At the end of the day, do I tend to talk more about things that didn't work out than things that did work out?

What about today has improved on yesterday?

What about this year is better than last year?

What relationships in life can I be grateful for?

What incidents have happened that I am so glad for?

What am I most thankful for about the city and country I live in?

What do I appreciate about my work life?

What parts of me would I not want to change and feel grateful for?

What activities in my life that I engage in and enjoy am I thankful for?

What artists, musicians, writers and other creatives do I enjoy and appreciate?

How could showing gratitude prevent burnout?

Challenge

Gratitude Ritual

Have a special notebook handy and make this challenge a bedtime ritual. Every night for a month, finish off your day by reflecting on what you are thankful for that day. Think of three to five different gratitudes and write them down in your notebook. Write about them in detail, also reflecting on how you feel and the associated emotions. The trick here is to think of different gratitudes every single day, no matter how big or small. If you do this for a month, you might have 150 different things you look back on that you have shown appreciation for that month. How cool!

Commitment

Going forward,
I commit to
these new rituals
to cultivate
more gratitude
in my life...

Notes

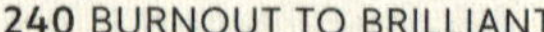

Practise Change

'Change is hard at first, messy in the middle and gorgeous in the end.'

ROBIN SHARMA

I DON'T KNOW about you, but I feel that change used to be slow. Summers were long, I always knew who was number one in the music charts and I could keep up with advances in technology. I was always the 'tech head' in my house growing up in the 80s and the first to know what was going on with the updates on our devices. I knew how to plug in the VCR and hook it up to the TV. I was the one who could power up the Commodore 64 computer and teach my parents how to use it. I was also the one who taught everyone how to use a mobile phone, back when they were the size of bricks. But nowadays, I feel like I don't know anything.

Everything moves so quickly now; my tech products send me messages every day to update them, I have *no idea* how to plug in anything to do with my TV and God only knows who is number one on the music charts now. I don't even know how old I am anymore. I've been sticking to the same age for the past few years because I can't be bothered doing the calculations. Change used to be slow and incremental. It felt like we had more time to keep up.

Today, it's rapid, radical and unpredictable, and many of us are distressed as a result of it.

In the workplace, we're business owners, short-term contractors, freelancers, consultants, entrepreneurs and transient workers. We're a part of the 'Great Resignation', but we're also 'quiet quitting' and, as a result, part of the 'Great Exhaustion'. There are more new terms around than ever. In the business world, we're talking VUCA and TUNA to describe the volatile, uncertain, novel and ambiguous world we live in.

There are so many moving parts, and our brains can't keep up with what could happen next. Unless we become psychologically adaptable and we move with change accordingly, we can feel overwhelmed and not able to keep up, which causes stress. Our brain isn't made for constant changes, but if we predict that change is going to continue, we can prepare our brain for being flexible and adaptable to whatever changes lay ahead. Going forward, we need to get used to change, be adaptable to what is going on in the context of our lives and be prepared to pivot.

Holding on to the emotions associated with the psychological resistance to change will exhaust us. Look at what happened during the pandemic: there were so many disruptions, so many imposed changes when we weren't quite ready and so many people felt fearful of what could be – particularly when they couldn't predict what was going to happen. Burnout is higher than ever after the pandemic, and it certainly is not just work-related. It's everything-related. When we are part of a global community of people who are chronically stressed, fearful, disrupted, uncertain, experiencing a lack of control, feeling disconnected and dealing with massive imposed societal changes that they are finding hard to navigate, we are going to get a more burned-out society. But change isn't going anywhere. It's here to stay.

For us to live our best life (at work and at home), we need to be adaptable. An adaptable mindset has proven to be a great measure against change. Being adaptable can make it easier to embrace disruption in the future and defuse the psychological impact it has on us. It's a mindset that enables us to continuously upgrade as our ways of living change in the future.

High levels of adaptability mean we can handle change better, and therefore we're more likely to be less affected when things inevitably change in the future (inevitably means it *will* happen). Adaptive thinking involves the ability to recognise unexpected situations, quickly consider various ways of responding and decide on the best step forward in real time (without being emotionally driven). So, how do we become more adaptable? How do we prepare for a world that will change constantly? How can we be resilient when life pivots us in a direction that we don't want to pivot in? We need to prepare. To be adaptable, we need to start practising. Preparing to pivot at any time means we need to practise change – starting now.

We need to get out of our comfort zone more often and do things that scare us a little bit. We need to challenge ourselves with different and new activities. We need to follow thought leaders we don't usually agree with, read books by authors we don't usually like and listen to the lyrics of the songs of musicians we've never listened to. We need to be open to different things and move away from the confirmation bias that steers our tastes, beliefs and ways of thinking.

We need to surround ourselves with inspiration. Look at and learn from people who've gone through what we're going through, and learn how they transformed. Be inspired by people who are doing what we aspire to do in the future. Follow their thoughts, read their autobiographies and listen to their stories. They are usually a lot more like us than we think. In a media world that often regurgitates the same stuff over and over again, purposefully look out for new insights, new research and new findings. Read up on the stories of possibilities and steer clear of doomscrolling.

We need to travel and broaden our minds. Ideally outside of our own culture, but if we can't travel too far, we should go somewhere we've never been before in our local area. We need to explore and wander around new places. I have, on many occasions, suggested to clients who are stuck in the same routine to go to a different shopping centre each week instead of the same one, just to mix it up a bit. The more new things we try and the more different places we go, the more our brain lights up as it absorbs all the sensory information from the external world, rather than being stuck at home entertaining our internal world. We need to spend more time with people who are different to us.

We need to adopt a growth mindset and view every change, every stuff-up and every mistake as an opportunity to learn more. We need to give our brain the chance to build resilience, by allowing ourselves to get in trouble a bit, get stressed, feel fear and get through it.

We need to inoculate ourselves now for future change. Then, if we find ourselves stuck in a tough situation where someone changes something at work or we go through something hard in life, we have built a resilient mind to get through it more easily.

Psychological adaptability is about riding the waves of change, no matter how strong the winds are. Standing up against the force of the wind and trying to resist it will burn us out.

Moving along with it and trusting where it's going will help us flow to where we need to be.

Considerations

How do I feel when change happens?

Is change easy when it is my idea?

Is change difficult when it is imposed on me?

Am I resistant to change? How do I act when change happens?

Do I become difficult when someone changes something?

What could I do to practise change?

Do I need to work on my problem-solving skills?

Am I quite close-minded? Do I need to be more open-minded?

Does my ego get in the way sometimes when change happens?

Do I push myself out of my comfort zone enough?

Do I try new things regularly or am I set in my ways?

How could practising change more prevent burnout?

Challenge

Try Something New

Think of something that you've always wanted to do in this one wild and precious life. It needs to be something that you can do in your local area and that is affordable (we don't need any excuses for you not to do this). Maybe it's learning to play a new instrument, learning a new language or joining a sporting club of a sport you don't know how to play. It will be uncomfortable, you won't know how to do it and you won't know anyone there to help you. Then, you are going to start it! You are going to be open to something new, and you are going to find your way there without any help. C'mon, you can do it! When you're there, and you've tried it out, notice how it feels.

Commitment

Going forward, I commit to these new rituals to help embrace change in my life...

Notes

Live Authentically

'To be yourself in a world that is constantly trying to make you something else is the greatest accomplishment.'

RALPH WALDO EMERSON

EARLIER ON IN my career I had a lovely client, Donna, who was well into a difficult separation from her partner and was going solo with the children. Her ex-boyfriend wasn't able to look after the children, and Donna did not have any family or friends to support her, as she moved away from her hometown years prior and had little contact with her loved ones. Feeling exhausted emotionally and physically from the daily parenting routine without any sort of reprieve, ongoing sleep deprivation, stressors surrounding an unstable ex-partner and ongoing financial stressors from not being able to work, Donna was in a constant state of anxiety, and felt she had nowhere to turn.

Donna and I met weekly and as she started feeling a little less anxious and more in control of her world, we started moving our sessions to fortnightly and then monthly. A lot of our sessions involved her debriefing about different issues that were cropping up, but speaking out loud to someone other than her little kids also enabled her to take some time for herself – to make sense of, process and think about what needed to happen next with the goings-on in her life.

One of the interesting parts of our interactions was that Donna was nearly the same age as me and was going through similar difficulties as I was at the time. Us psychologists are human, after all (go figure). We're not immune to the trials and tribulations of life that all our clients go through. Separation, divorce, sickness, grief, financial stressors, even mental health issues – we've got you covered. But alas, you'd often never know for a few reasons: a) we're not supposed to be sharing our personal information with you (unless, on occasion, it's particularly relevant and helpful); b) I'm sure you're not paying us to talk about ourselves; and c) we often have barely enough time in sessions to talk about your issues, never mind our issues. But seriously, on many occasions I have wanted to share more of my personal story with clients, particularly when they are going through similar adversities that I have successfully navigated. It's almost like ... here's some therapy that is grounded in ten years of training, but here's a bonus real story because you're likely to remember that more.

With Donna, this happened without intention. One evening after work I was sitting on the river foreshore having a picnic dinner with my young children, and my kids headed over to the playground. Some other kids were playing on the slide at the same time, and inevitably all of them ended up running around together. As I walked over, I realised the parent was Donna. Usually when I see clients out in public, they either run in the other direction or it becomes a little awkward and they look away, particularly when someone is with them. Not everyone tells their significant others that they are seeing a psychologist, so it's always best to err on the side of caution and pretend you don't know them – unless they approach you, of course. But Donna yelled out 'hello', and we got chatting for a bit. It was nothing deep, just a bit of playground mum banter about the kids and then we went our separate ways.

I didn't see Donna for a year or so after that, but when she did come in for a consult, she mentioned that she'd been doing well and that a big turning point for her was seeing me alone with my two kids that day. She said that she went home that evening feeling less alone in her own story. She felt a sort of kinship that had been lacking in her world. The fact that her psychologist was working and raising two kids by herself meant that she could do that too. And that's what she had been busy doing, not needing any sessions for a long while.

When Donna revealed that to me, it became a turning point for me, too. It made me think that people need to hear more stories of what others are going through and that, more than ever, we need to share our real stories to develop a connection around our humanness. When others around us demonstrate authenticity, we feel less alone in our stories.

A lot of us have been wearing a social mask to please society for most of our lives, which has become a fictional self that we have been presenting to the world whenever we have people around us. And because we often have people around us telling us who we're supposed to be, a slow slipping away of who we once were can take place. It's time for this to stop.

When we think of the word 'honest', we think it's about not lying. We also think about it in terms of what we expect from other people – truthfulness, sincerity and, of course, not being deceitful to us. But it's so much more than that. And, most importantly, we need to look at the honesty that resides within ourselves – and then align our behaviours to fit. As Eckhart Tolle said, 'Only the truth of who you are, if realized, will set you free.'

Learning to be real again, learning to be ourselves – remembering and perhaps even returning to who we were a long time ago – is where we feel most at ease. It's about giving ourselves permission to be a piece of non-fiction, an ever-changing piece of work, that is constantly responding to, flowing with and changing as a result of the world in which we exist.

One of the interesting things about authenticity is

that it involves baring our soul a little and sharing parts of ourselves that we have kept hidden. It means sharing our daily struggles and the associated negative emotions. It may involve sharing stories of times we have felt shame or guilt. It may bring up old wounds. It involves mistakes, failures and errors in judgement. It allows us to share who we really are, what we really want in life, who we want to show up as and what we want to do in this world. Revealing this and *being* this is therapeutic. It lifts a weight off our chest and, funnily enough, connects us to our fellow human beings.

In terms of mental health and wellbeing, and the feelings of stress, anxiety and pressure that so often lead to burnout, the more real we are about our struggles with our mental health, the closer we are to getting help. Being authentic and sharing with those around us how we feel and why we might be feeling like that helps open us to more possibilities about what we can do to recover and heal from the issues that we are dealing with.

Authenticity also creates an increased awareness in society about what people need. Keeping our feelings quiet and keeping our thoughts to ourselves doesn't create the change the world so desperately needs. When more people are authentic, it gives the world the data it needs to make changes on a grander scale – this doesn't happen when we fake or filter our way through life. Being authentic helps us, and it helps others.

If we're authentic, the people who are not right for us will drop away, and the right people and opportunities will enter our life. We will experience more flow than we ever have before. Being authentic will involve being less perfect than society prescribes, but once we settle into this, it will remove the pressure and set us free – free to chart waters that we never thought possible.

When we're authentic and we own all parts of us, we can then have the confidence to shine as the person we really are. We can only shine sustainably when we have enough energy to do so. And when we shine, we can light up others around us. Funnily enough, the word 'brilliant' comes from the French word for 'shining'. See, burnout can make you brilliant.

Considerations

Am I showing up as who I really am?

What parts of me am I hiding? Why am I hiding them?

What experiences that I have gone through in my life am I not sharing?

What am I afraid will happen if I share these experiences with certain people?

How will I feel if I don't share my story, along with what I think and feel about it?

How could sharing my stories benefit me?

How could sharing my stories benefit others?

If I had nothing to lose, what would I share with the world?

Who in my life could I be more vulnerable with?

Where can I show up more authentically in my life?

How could showing up authentically prevent burnout?

Challenge

Deep Conversations

Think of someone you are in a relationship with – it might be a partner, a parent, a friend or even a colleague. Now, think of something about you that you think of often, that you haven't told that person, which still affects you deeply. If it still affects you, it is likely to be affecting your relationship with this person, too. The next time you are in a deep conversation with this person and you feel it's the right time, slowly and gently give more of yourself in the conversation. Using 'I' statements, share your stories along with the fears you've felt in keeping these things to yourself. Notice how this is not only therapeutic for you (and a big emotional release), but how it facilitates a deeper connection with the other person.

Commitment

Going forward,
I commit to
these new rituals
to encourage
living more
authentically ...

Notes

EPILOGUE

Onwards

'You have brains in your head. You have feet in your shoes. You can steer yourself any direction you choose.'

DR SEUSS

THIS YEAR WAS tough. Tougher than the one before. Tougher than the one before that, which started me on my journey to needing to be in water. I did establish that there was perhaps a reason or two for this. Maybe it was because I had worked too much again, as psychologists tend to do. Maybe it was the result of an excessive workload that was sometimes a little hard to keep up with. Maybe it was because of ongoing demands on my time from the too many hats I wear. Maybe it was because of the overwhelming demands plus the guilt around caring for an elderly, unwell parent. Maybe it was because every single night of the week I was driving teenagers to all their sports trainings and work commitments. Maybe it was that a few more loved ones passed away. Maybe it was because of my beloved cat who didn't make it, which totally broke my heart. Maybe it's because I felt that I kept letting people down because it's impossible to be in three or four places at once. Maybe it was because certain people I was working with were causing me stress and pressure. Maybe it was perimenopause knocking at the door (yes, still). Maybe it was because of all of it.

But this time, I noticed it. And, as a result, the stressors didn't build up. (I didn't trip up my staircase, either ... not once.) This year, I feel less exhausted overall and healthier than ever. I have more clarity in what I want from life and what I want to create in it. I feel calmer and more confident in my ability to tackle life and all that it throws at me.

This wasn't because this year was perfect and all went well. A lot of it was tough and moments were soaked in emotions that were quite hard to shift. Some of these emotions involved imposed stressors, some were lingering ones that had been around for a while and some came out of left field. But, at the same time as these stressors arrived and then, over time, subsided, self-care rituals increased right alongside them and helped me along the way. The warm showers became longer, the dog walks became more frequent, more boundaries were raised, more sunsets were watched, more books were read and 'no' was said more.

Don't get me wrong, there have been times where the pressure of a large workload has built up a little too much, where excessive tiredness has got the better of me. There have been times where I've dealt with individuals who have made me think that people living alone in a forest with 30 cats are actually onto a good thing. This is normal and it was fleeting. But some incredibly wonderful things happened at the same time. For starters, I wouldn't be writing this book if a few little awesome moments didn't happen along the way. Yes, life can get tough, but we need a healthy foundation and the right psychological capabilities to ride through it.

For all of us, life will be full of difficult moments. For some, it will be tough moments for them as individuals during their childhood. For others, their adversities won't come until later in life. For some, the individual adversities never seem to go away. Sometimes, those adversities are peppered across the timeline of a life, with the space to try to process the necessary emotions along the way. Other times, it's almost like the universe decides to dump them all at once, with no time to make sense of anything.

As a collective, we can all experience the feelings associated with the impact of one global crisis after another. And, of course, we can be living through collective adversity *and* our individual adversities at the same time.

But the golden nugget in all of this is that we need to *feel*. We need to notice our reactions to these events we are a part of, witnessing, hearing about or experiencing. We need to give ourselves the space to notice the effect it is having on our lives, our mind and our body. Then, we can take control of what we can, pivot when we need to, change what we want to and stop when we need to.

We need to feel the impact of life being tough. We need to feel the chest pain in our grief, we need to feel the dread in anxiety, we need to feel the panic in our fears and we need to feel the mind-boggling numbness in boredom. Then, we need to choose new ways of being so we don't get stuck in those feelings. We need to use those important emotions to lean into what we want next in our life so that we can feel less of those feelings and align more to the feelings that feel so much better. The happiness, the joy, the accomplishment, the surprise, the awe, the nostalgia, the calmness, the contentment and the *brilliance*.

In these volatile, uncertain, complex and ambiguous times, where we can be affected by not only what is directly happening to us or those close to us but also what millions of people are going through right now, there's never been a better time to learn how to manage our own mental health to prevent ourselves getting to breaking point. We can be not feeling okay for a few minutes, an hour or even a day. But we're not supposed to be not feeling okay for weeks, months or years.

Our emotions are temporary if we listen to them. Time does help us heal and we are stronger than we think. Life will get difficult and we will react to things. But we need to listen to what we need, feel what needs to be felt, ponder as to why, adjust the sails and move towards a life that's way better than it ever was before.

Burnout Blueprint

Date: ____________________

Goals: What do I want to make sure I achieve this month? (E.g. exercise, relaxation, meditation, socialising, saying 'no' more.)

Why: Why does this achievement matter to me?

Actions: What micro steps do I need to take to achieve these goals? (Be as specific as you can. E.g. the behaviour, when you will do it, how much you will do, etc.)

1.
2.
3.
4.
5.

Help: List any people you need support from, clubs/ organisations you need to join, appointments you need to make or resources you need to get hold of to achieve these goals.

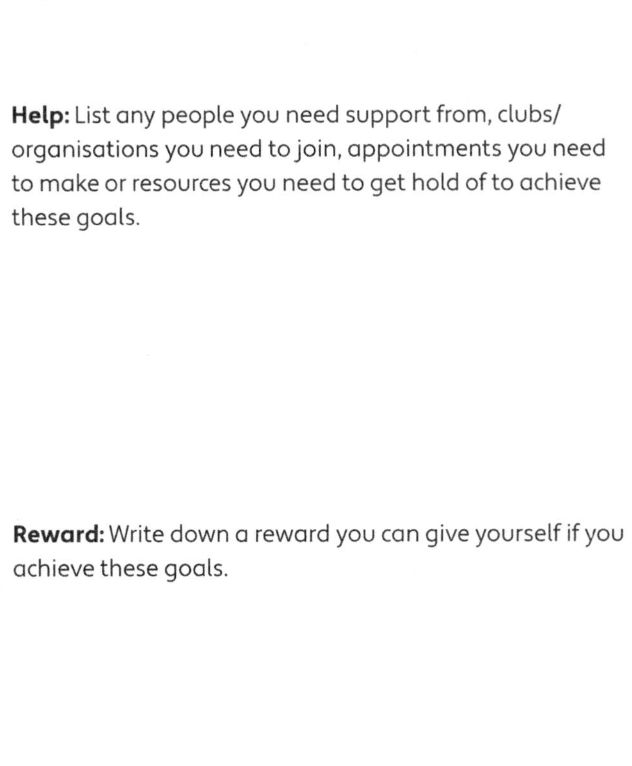

Reward: Write down a reward you can give yourself if you achieve these goals.

Reflections: Journal about how you went this month, what your achievements were, what your roadblocks were, what new changes need to happen and what advice you could give yourself for next month.

References

1. World Health Organization (WHO), 2019. ICD-11: *International Classification of Diseases for Mortality and Morbidity Statistics*, https://icd.who.int/en
2. Bianchi, R., Mayor, E., Schonfeld, I.S. and Laurent, E., 2018. 'Burnout and depressive symptoms are not primarily linked to perceived organizational problems.' *Psychology, Health & Medicine*, Vol. 23(9), https://doi.org/10.1080/13548506.2018.1476725
3. Roskam, I., Raes, M. and Mikolajczak, M., 2017. 'Exhausted parents: Development and preliminary validation of the parental burnout inventory.' *Frontiers in Psychology*, Vol. 8, https://doi.org/10.3389/fpsyg.2017.00163
4. Dyrbye, L.N., Shanafelt, T.D., Johnson, P.O. et al., 2019. 'A cross-sectional study exploring the relationship between burnout, absenteeism, and job performance among American nurses.' *BMC Nursing*, Vol. 18, https://doi.org/10.1186/s12912-019-0382-7
5. Mohren, D.C., Swaen, G.M., Kant, I.J. et al., 2003. 'Common infections and the role of burnout in a Dutch working population.' *Journal of Psychosomatic Research*, Vol. 55(3), https://doi.org/10.1016/S0022-3999(02)00517-2

6. Stojanovich, L. and Marisavljevich, D., 2008. 'Stress as a trigger of autoimmune disease.' *Autoimmune Review*, Vol. 7(3), https://doi.org/10.1016/j.autrev.2007.11.007
7. Armon, G., Melamed, S., Shirom, A. and Shapira, I., 2010. 'Elevated burnout predicts the onset of musculoskeletal pain among apparently healthy employees.' *Journal of Occupational Health Psychology*, Vol. 15(4), https://doi.org/10.1037/a0020726
8. Hall, N.C., Lee, S.Y. and Rahimi, S., 2019. 'Self-efficacy, procrastination, and burnout in post-secondary faculty: An international longitudinal analysis.' *PLOS ONE*, Vol. 14(12), https://doi.org/10.1371/journal.pone.0226716
9. Federici, R.A. and Skaalvik, E.M., 2012. 'Principal self-efficacy: relations with burnout, job satisfaction and motivation to quit.' *Social Psychology Education*, Vol. 15, https://doi.org/10.1007/s11218-012-9183-5
10. Albulescu, P., Macsinga, I., Rusu, A., Sulea, C., Bodnaru, A. et al., 2022. 'Give me a break!' A systematic review and meta-analysis on the efficacy of micro-breaks for increasing well-being and performance. *PLOS ONE*, Vol. 17(8), https://doi.org/10.1371/journal.pone.0272460
11. Tseng, J. and Poppenk, J., 2020. 'Brain meta-state transitions demarcate thoughts across task contexts exposing the mental noise of trait neuroticism.' *Nature Communications*, Vol. 11, https://doi.org/10.1038/s41467-020-17255-9
12. Toussaint, L., Nguyen, Q.A., Roettger, C., Dixon, K., Offenbächer, M., Kohls, N., Hirsch, J. and Sirois, F., 2021.

'Effectiveness of progressive muscle relaxation, deep breathing, and guided imagery in promoting psychological and physiological states of relaxation.' *Evidence-Based Complementary and Alternative Medicine,* Vol. 2021, https://doi.org/10.1155/2021/5924040/

13. Salmon, P., 2001. 'Effects of physical exercise on anxiety, depression, and sensitivity to stress: a unifying theory.' *Clinical Psychology Review,* Vol. 21(1), https://doi.org/10.1016/S0272-7358(99)00032-X
14. Ruisoto, P., Ramírez, M.R., García, P.A., Paladines-Costa, B., Vaca, S.L. and Clemente-Suárez, V.J., 2021. 'Social support mediates the effect of burnout on health in health care professionals.' *Frontiers in Psychology,* Vol. 11, https://doi.org/10.3389/fpsyg.2020.623587
15. Petelczyc, C.A., Capezio, A., Wang, L., Restubog, S.L.D. and Aquino, K., 2018. 'Play at work: An integrative review and agenda for future research.' *Journal of Management,* Vol. 44(1), https://doi.org/10.1177/0149206317731519
16. Van Vleet, M., and Feeney, B. C., 2015. 'Young at Heart: A perspective for advancing research on play in adulthood.' *Perspectives on Psychological Science,* Vol. 10(5), https://doi.org/10.1177/1745691615596789
17. Lin, C. C., 2017. 'The effect of higher-order gratitude on mental well-being: Beyond personality and unifactoral gratitude.' *Current Psychology,* Vol. 36, https://doi.org/10.1007/s12144-015-9392-0

18. Enmons, R. A. and McCullough, M. E., 2003. 'Counting blessings versus burdens: An experimental investigation of gratitude and subjective well-being in daily life.' *Journal of Personality and Social Psychology*, Vol. 84(2), https://doi.org/10.1037/0022-3514.84.2.377
19. Krentzman, A. R., 2017. 'Gratitude, abstinence, and alcohol use disorders: Report of a preliminary finding.' *Journal of Substance Abuse Treatment*, Vol. 78, https://doi.org/10.1016/j.jsat.2017.04.013

Acknowledgements

Firstly, thank you to Simone Landes, who saw my writing potential and guided me in the right direction to make this book a possibility. Thank you to Kelly Doust, Elizabeth Robinson-Griffith and the rest of the team at Affirm Press for liking this idea, seeing this as an important issue that would resonate and swiftly guiding me through my first publishing journey.

Thank you to my family and friends, who are always there to support, and lend an ear to, the many, many ideas that I'm keen to turn into reality. Never underestimate the importance of our long coast walks, lingering dinners and the chats over a cheeky prosecco.

I'd like to acknowledge the hundreds of people I've had the privilege to work with over the years. I've learned and continue to learn about the human condition through your stories.

Thank you to my beautiful kids, Lali and Luca, who simply by 'being' inspire me every day. And of course, my fur baby, Chilly, my antidote to stress. Without our long, wandering walks in nature, this book would not have been written.